D1453774

The Aleph Weaver:
Biblical, Kabbalistic and Judaic Elements in Borges

The Aleph Weaver:

Biblical, Kabbalistic and Judaic Elements in Borges

Edna Aizenberg

Scripta humanistica

*PQ
1797
.B635
Z53*

Publisher and Distributor:
SCRIPTA HUMANISTICA
1383 Kersey Lane
Potomac, Maryland 20854 U.S.A.

Contents

v

Introduction

Borges is an Aleph weaver. His texts, so rich in cultural allusions and in symbolic import, show a particular predilection for the heritage of the Aleph: Bible, Kabbalah, Judaism. In his varied writings Borges weaves and unweaves this heritage, using textual strategies and archetypal metaphors derived from Jewish sources.

While Borges's interest in what he calls *lo hebreo*, the Judaic, has been recognized as a significant aspect of his work, it has not been the object of a comprehensive study. By this I mean a study which inquires into the reasons for Borges's Aleph-making—his fascination with Judaism—and at the same time examines not only the Kabbalah in Borges, but other meaningful Judaic strands as well. My book is an attempt to do these things. In it, I look at the personal, historical and cultural circumstances which shaped the author's approach to *lo hebreo*; consider some of his less-known texts on the subject; and discuss his handling of Judaically-based discursive techniques and myths.

Borges's fondness for *lo hebreo* is hardly typical in Latin-American literature, so I felt it was important to elucidate the origins and development of this apparently arcane inclination. What my inquiry reveals, I believe, is that unusual as it may seem, Borges's interest in Jewish culture is in fact a function of an essential characteristic and problematic of Latin-American culture: the deep involvement with Europe coupled with a sense of otherness vis-à-vis the Continent and the Western order it represents. The chronicle of Borges's fascination with *lo hebreo* is by and large the chronicle of a Latin American whose European connections and concern for Western civilization led him to Judaism, and for whom Judaism became a paradigm for being Latin American. Many elements of the Judaic heritage and the Jewish condition which attract Borges derive from this double movement, and the first part of my study traces how that came about. In the process, the author is revealed as a man and an intellectual actively reacting to people and events, whose writings include more than one engagé text, and whose creation of fictive worlds in his stories—contrary to some of his detractors—does not imply an unawareness of reality.

To elaborate the portrait of Borges as an admirer of *lo hebreo*, I have gathered information from a variety of sources: biographies of the author; oral and written testimonies by close friends and fellow intellectuals; and historical and cultural studies of Borges's times. I have also employed Borges's own articles and essays, interviews—including a long personal interview I had with him in December, 1979—poetry and fictional works. This Borgesian material is interesting not only because it provides facts which are supported and supplemented by outside sources, but also because it reveals a personal vision: the image of the Judaic as the author sees it and as he would have us see it. By citing his preferred writers, works and themes, and laying bare his private mythologies— mythologies that occasionally have to be adjusted in light of other information—Borges delineates a space in which he wants his literature read. Taken together, the authorial and nonauthorial materials offer a rather complete picture, a picture that balances subjective views with critical studies.

The second part of my book focuses exclusively on Borges's works. I analyze how a literary innovator works with the cultural legacy of his precursors, indeed, how he innovates by manipulating bits and pieces of that legacy. Since the major axes around which Borges organizes his writing are the esthetic use of religious ideas and the retelling of time-honored tales, he not surprisingly finds antecedents for his "novel," contemporary literature in such sources as Scripture and the Kabbalah. I point out what these antecedents are, more broadly, as they are reflected in Borges's narrative philosophy, and more specifically, as a number of topoi he reelaborates in his fictional writings. To do this, in addition to expanding on the work of other scholars, I have built on my discoveries of unnoted Borgesiana, for example, texts on the Book of Job and Spinoza.

The mention of Spinoza brings me to a question: how do I define a Jewish element in Borges? The allusions to the Kabbalah or the use of kabbalistic ideas are obviously Judaic; so are the poems to Israel. Can the same be said of the biblical threads in Borges's writing? The Hebrew Scriptures are the patrimony not only of Jews, but of Christians and nonbelievers, and certain parts of the Bible are not accepted or canonized by Judaism. Does quoting Scripture, then, constitute a Jewish element? And what of the references to Spinoza, Heine or some of the German Expressionist poets, excommunicated, converted or marginal Jews whose works are not always—and in a number of cases rarely—Judaic in content? Is their presence in Borges a Jewish one?

As far as Borges is concerned, Holy Writ, Spinoza's speculations, Heine's writings, and the poetry of the German Expressionists all belong to the orbit of Judaism. This definition of Jewishness, idiosyncratic or questionable as it may be, is in fact largely supported by public perception. To cite just two examples: Spinoza is most often portrayed as a "Jewish genius" despite his offical excommunication from the Amsterdam Judeo-Sephardi community, and German Expressionism was called a Jewish movement before Borges. Borges accepted and built on these characterizations, rejecting dissenting ones, because they suited his ends, the reading of *lo hebreo* that he would like us to carry away from his texts. The same is true of certain intellectual postures—for instance, irreverent innovativeness—which, beyond specific authors and writings, Borges considers Judaic. Judaism as here defined is, then, a wide spectrum, centered in Borges's own perceptions, yet confirmed by a consensus albeit not universal, definitely broad.

Since my study is crosscultural and may be of interest not only to Hispanists, I have translated many of the shorter quotations from Borges into English, thus leaving enough Spanish to give the flavor of the original, but at the same time making it easier for the non-Hispanist to follow the flow of the text.

Several people deserve my thanks for their support during the writing of this study. Professor Ana María Barrenechea was a constant source of encouragement and knowledge—Borgesian and otherwise; Billy Thompson provided me with valuable advice, and more valuable criticism; my husband, Joshua, was at all times the wonderful companion, patient listener and diligent proofreader every author needs; and my boys, Gabriel and Salo, were the most tolerant of sons, sharing their mother with Borges for many long months.

I would also like to thank Rear Admiral Floyd H. Miller, President of the State University of New York-Maritime College, Dr. William R. Porter, Vice-President for Academic Affairs, and the Maritime College Foundation for generously awarding me a grant which helped make the publication of my book possible. I am likewise indebted to Dr. Joel J. Belson, Chairman of the Humanities Department, for his efforts on behalf of this project.

Finally, Borges himself also deserves a debt of gratitude for patiently answering my questions during our interview and our shorter conversations in New York and Buenos Aires, and for his masterful texts, without which this study would not have been written.

PART I

1. *Bilingualism and Biblicism*

Why is Borges interested in Judaism? A good place to begin the search for an answer is the Buenos Aires household into which he was born in 1899.

It is a home with "two codes," one Spanish, the other English.[1] At the simplest level, this just means that both languages were spoken by the part-Argentine, part-British Borges clan, a not atypical mixture deriving from the immigrant character of Argentine society. But the dualism of tongues had greater implications. First, each linguistic code reflected a distinct family history and, as a result, differences in certain socio-cultural attributes and attitudes; and second, each linguistic code with its attendant characteristics formed the nucleus of what Ricardo Piglia has called Borges's "biographic fable," the representation of his background that Borges has evolved into a kind of authorized version.[2] In this

---

[1] Emir Rodríguez Monegal, *Jorge Luis Borges: A Literary Biography* (New York: Dutton, 1978), p. 21. This is the most up-to-date and complete biography of the author. In it, Rodríquez Monegal discusses the importance of these two codes extensively.

[2] Ricardo Piglia, "Ideología y ficción en Borges," *Punto de vista*, 2, No. 5 (March 1979), 3–6.

version the very real contrasts and dissonances which existed between the Spanish and English codes were molded into a schematized system of oppositions: what was present on one side was absent on the other (Piglia, p. 4). A contrastive summary of the two codes, seen through the lens of Borges's interpretation, would look like this:[3]

HISPANO-ARGENTINE	ANGLO-ARGENTINE
Mother: Leonor Acevedo de Borges	Father: Jorge Guillermo Borges Haslam
Descended from old Creole families (Acevedo/Laprida/ Suárez) established in America since time of the Spanish conquest.	Descended from old Creole families, but mother, Fanny Haslam Arnett, came from Staffordshire, England. Mother's elder sister married an Italian Jew, Jorge Suárez. This couple brought Fanny to Argentina.
Hero worship toward military ancestors who took part in independence struggle and subsequent civil wars.	Not so devoted to memory of heroic ancestors.
Spanish: language spoken by mother, relegated to domestic concerns; language of servants.	English: language spoken by British grandmother who lived with the Borgeses, considered vehicle of culture, a sign of an open, hospitable mind. Jorge Luis reads English before Spanish; does much of reading in father's English library.
Catholic, traditional piety. "Protestant" considered a synonym of "Jew," "atheist," or "heretic."	Grandmother: Protestant, knew Bible by heart in English. Father: liberal, agnostic, skeptic; interested in metaphysics and mysticism; initiated Jorge Luis into love of philosophy in general and Spinoza in particular.[4]

---

[3] The information in this summary appears in Rodríguez Monegal's biography, particularly pp. 5, 7, 10–11, 17–19 and 51.

[4] In an interview which appears in *Homenaje a Baruch Spinoza* (Buenos Aires: Museo Judío de Buenos Aires, 1976), a volume issued to commemorate

4

What the comparison reveals is a heterodox streak running through the British-paternal side of the family, which provides the Protestants, Jews, (free) thinkers and metaphysical speculators among the Borges relations. The Hispano-maternal side, on the other hand, places more emphasis on its military heritage, and values orthodoxy over intellectualism.

This dichotomy has been mentioned by Borges in interviews;[5] it has also been woven into his fictions. In "There Are More Things," the narrator's uncle, Edwin Arnett (who possesses many qualities belonging to Borges's father, including the family name) is of British origin, undogmatic in religious matters and imbued with an intellectual-metaphysical curiosity which he passes on to his nephew (read son).[6] The antithesis, who appears in "La señora mayor," is the hundred-year-old María Justina Rubio de Jáuregui, daughter of a minor hero of Argentina's independence wars, a devout, unquestioning Catholic for whom Protestant, Jew, Mason and non-believer are all the same thing; a woman who is not unintelligent, but who has never enjoyed the pleasures of the mind.[7]

From the traits ascribed by Borges to "the old lady," it is clear that she is a projection of his view of the maternal Acevedo line. The detail of her longevity only cements this identification: Borges's mother was almost her age (94) at the time of the story's publication.

These two contrasting codes are, as noted earlier, a schematized version of the reality of the Borges household.

---

the 300th anniversary of the philosopher's death, Borges attributes his lasting interest in Spinoza to his father's influence (p. 49).

[5] See Jean de Milleret, *Entrevistas con Jorge Luis Borges* (Caracas: Monte Avila, 1970), pp. 163; 33.

[6] *El libro de arena* (Buenos Aires: Emecé, 1975), pp. 65–77.

[7] "La señora mayor," *Obras completas* (Buenos Aires: Emece, 1974), pp. 1048–52. Unless otherwise noted, quotations from the following works by Borges will come from the *Obras completas*, hereafter, *OC*: *Evaristo Carriego* [1930]; *Discusión* [1932]; *Historia universal de la infamia* [1935]; *Historia de la eternidad* [1936]; *Ficciones* [1944]; *El Aleph* [1949]; *Otras inquisiciones* [1952]; *El hacedor* [1960]; *El otro, el mismo* [1964]; *Para las seis cuerdas* [1965]; *Elogio de la sombra* [1969]; *El informe de Brodie* [1970]; *El oro de los tigres* [1972].)

5

They simplify that reality, being—to quote Borges's words from another context—a compound of "substantial truth and accidental errors" (*OC*, 743). Father, the parent with the international-Protestant-Jewish-intellectual connections, was a native of the "primitive" Argentine hinterland and the son of a fighting Creole colonel. Despite his library of English books, the one novel he wrote, *El caudillo* (1921), was quite autochthonous in character. Mother, portrayed by Borges as the product of a family so narrow-minded in its Catholicity that it considered being a Protestant identical with being a Jew or a freethinker, married a man with exactly these "taints"—indicating that the Acevedos were perhaps not so prejudiced after all. Though less devoted to learning than her husband, Doña Leonor nonetheless knew French as a young woman, later learned English and, unlike María Justina Rubio de Jáuregui, retained her lucidity well into old age.[8]

In spite of such inaccuracies, however, the two codes did capture the essential truth of Borges's family history. They condensed the central images of his background, images which he would absorb, embroider and expand into a worldview and a literature. And in these predominant images of Borges's formative years, Judaism was connected to that part of the soul worth cultivating.[9] It was related to open-mindedness, heterodoxy, cosmopolitanism. It also formed part of a posture of nonconformity, of a distancing from established norms. At this stage of his development Georgie—Borges's nickname as a child—likely had little contact with flesh-and-blood Jews, and had not yet done his extensive reading on Judaism. But the word "Jew" already had begun to take on a meaning which remained fairly consistent throughout his long career. And that meaning—like so much else in Borges—over-

---

[8] This information about Doña Leonor is culled from Milleret, p. 164 and María Esther Vázquez, *Borges: imágenes, memorias, diálogos* (Caracas: Monte Avila, 1977), pp. 21 and 40.

[9] Borges has also cultivated the other side of his inheritance—the fighting, man-of-action side—but he has done so in literature, not in reality. Thus, for him, the part of the soul really worth cultivating is the "Jewish" part, which has absorbed the other, turning it from truth to textuality.

turned tradition. The Jew, with few exceptions, is a positive figure, not an object of opprobrium and denigration.

In later life the dualism which the Borges home fostered as well as the idea of Jewishness it proposed was extended to include society at large. It seems that Father, the parent with both the bicultural background and the "Jewish" characteristics, was the one to suggest this wider application to the son who idolized and imitated him. Interpreting San Martín's dictum, "You will be what you have to be or you will be nothing," during a conversation with Georgie, Father projects the phrase, which is couched in individual terms, into a collective characterization, a nutshell sociology of Argentina:

> 'Serás lo que debes ser' —serás un caballero, un católico, un argentino, un miembro del Jockey Club, un admirador de Uriburu, un admirador de los extensos rústicos de Quirós— 'y si no, no serás nada' —serás un israelita, un anarquista, un mero guarango, un auxiliar primero; la Comisión Nacional de Cultura ignorará tus libros. . .[10]

On the one hand there is the Establishment view of what it meant to be Argentine. It is essentially synonymous with membership in the ruling oligarchy, possessors of blue blood and wealth, whose bastion and refuge from the immigrant masses—among them Jews—was the exclusive Jockey Club; whose politics were represented by General Uriburu, an advocate of Mussolini who in 1930 overthrew the populist Irigoyen; and whose artistic ideal was the nostalgic glorification of a disappearing rural way of life. On the other hand there is the counterview, the anti-Establishment Argentina of the not-so-rich and the poor, the foreign-born, workers, political and intellectual anarchists whose actions and writings did not bear the imprimatur of official circles.[11] These are identified as "Jews" in opposition to the Catholics of the privileged band,

---

[10] Jorge Luis Borges, "Respuesta a la encuesta entre los escritores," *Latitud* (Buenos Aires), No. 1 (Feb. 1945), p. 4.

[11] For a discussion of the oligarchy and its attitudes and ideals, see David Viñas, *Literatura argentina y realidad política: apogeo de la oligarquía* (Buenos Aires: Siglo Veinte, 1975).

and it is with them that Jorge Guillermo Borges, though related to the Establishment by background, profession (law) and marriage obviously feels more in tune (*Biography*, p. 93). That the son accepted his father's framework is clear.[12] In practically every stage of his life, Borges saw Jewishness as the antithesis of what he regarded to be ultranationalism, religious intolerance and xenophobia. In some cases his reading of just who formed the anti-Jewish side was not totally accurate (as in the case of Perón, whom he saw as a Nazi Jew-baiter[13]), yet Borges inevitably stuck to the duality, finding, like Father, that his sympathies usually lay with *los israelitas*.[14]

But the sense of dualism fostered by the Borgeses did not only encourage the author's sympathy for Jews because it suggested a non- or anti-Jewish thesis and a Jewish antithesis; the sole fact of twoness, the coexistence in the household of two languages and all they implied, was advantageous for the development of Borges's interest in the patrimony of Israel. George Steiner, analyzing the relationship of language and literature in our time, notes the "linguistic pluralism or 'unhousedness' of certain great writers."[15] Borges figures prominently among these, along with Samuel Beckett and Vladi-

---

[12] The father-son conversation suggesting this framework comes from the time of Uriburu, which may also be the period when Borges began to work out his authorized version of the two codes. This was an era of fascist, anti-Semitic ascendency when Jewishness clearly represented the antithesis to the established philosophy, and a Manichaean scheme seemed particularly apt for making even sharper existing family differences in order to disassociate yourself from now-popular stances (religious intolerance, lack of intellectualism) and associate yourself with others (heterodoxy, pleasures of the mind).

[13] See Chapter 6 in the first part of this study where Borges's attitude to Perón is discussed at length.

[14] Piglia points out that Borges has retained a bipartite model of society throughout his life (p. 6). He also notes that the author's dualism, fostered by his double lineage, is reflected both in the ideology and the structure of his writings. (This would include the Jewish/anti-Jewish confrontations in Borges's stories as well as such structural devices as the oxymoron.) A study of these dualities can be found in Jaime Alazraqui, *Versiones. Inversiones. Reversiones. El espejo como modelo estructural del relato en los cuentos de Borges* (Madrid: Gredos, 1977).

[15] George Steiner, *Extraterritorial* (New York: Atheneum, 1971), p. viii.

8

mir Nabokov. Out of their fluency in more than one tongue flows their "extraterritoriality": a refusal to be tied down to a single heritage; a breadth of outlook that values multiple cultures; and a skepticism with respect to the givens of the language—and by extension of the cultures—in which their literature is produced (p. 11). The exposure to English as well as Spanish in childhood days provided Borges with his initial extraterritorial window. He himself has emphasized the broadening, liberalizing effects of such bilingualism:

> Si un hombre crece dentro de una sola cultura, si se habitúa a ver en los otros idiomas esa especie de dialectos hostiles o arbitrarios, todo eso tiene que estrechar su espíritu. Pero si un hombre se acostumbra a pensar en dos idiomas, y se acostumbra a pensar que el pasado de su mente son dos grandes literaturas, eso tiene que ser benéfico para él. [16]

Learning to think in two distinct ways, with which were associated two cultural traditions and even more than two patterns of belief (or disbelief), was beneficial for the future author. It taught him to appreciate various civilizations and to prize the different and uncanonical—all postures which favored a positive view of Judaism.

The Borges family's duality of tongues was important in forming the author's outlook on the Jewish heritage in still another way: it was the English-paternal code, the one already associated with Jewishness, that served as his earliest access to the texts of the Hebrew tradition. As Borges explains:

> . . .yo llegué muy pronto a ese venero, ese manantial [of Hebrew culture], porque una de mis abuelas era inglesa y sabía la Biblia de memoria. Alguien citaba una sentencia bíblica y ella daba inmediatamente el capítulo y el versículo. Como yo me he criado dentro de la lengua castellana y dentro de la lengua inglesa, la Biblia entró en mí muy tempranamente. [17]

For Borges—as these words indicate—the Bible is an essen-

---

[16] Rita Guibert, "Borges habla de Borges," *Life en español*, 31, No. 5, 11 March 1968, 48–60 rpt. in *Jorge Luis Borges*, ed. Jaime Alazraqui (Madrid: Taurus, 1976), pp. 318–355. The quote appears on p. 350.

[17] "Los primeros 25 años de *Davar*," *Davar* (Buenos Aires), No. 125 (Spring 1974), p. 71.

tially Hebrew book. Fanny Haslam's knowledge and love of Scripture, an example of English-Protestant culture's deep-rooted biblicism, became one more source for the appreciation of Judaism. Part of Borges's British legacy was a high regard for Holy Writ, a regard that almost all Englishmen had irrespective of their individual degree of orthodoxy. The widespread availability of the Bible in the vernacular thanks to a series of scriptural translations (some apparently found in the Borges home[18]) made the "English, perhaps more than any other people in Europe . . . Bible *readers.*"[19] It also had a lasting influence on Protestant morality and on English literature. When Borges calls the Hebrew Bible "the point of departure for everything," referring to it as the foundation of Western ethics and as one of the ur-texts of Western literature, he is reflecting the inheritance of his Scripture-quoting British grandmother.[20]

Borges's formative years in Buenos Aires had suggested an approach to Jews and Judaism. In a home with two codes, which promoted the growth of a feeling of twoness, proposing alternative paths, Jewishness became attractive as the less-trodden, but richer path, the one that led forward to the unestablished and the uncharted as well as backward to the origin. But these youthful beginnings had to be reinforced and built upon before they could mature into a clear vision. In 1914, the Borges family left Argentina to begin seven years of residence in Europe. This Continental experience strengthened the extraterritorial vein in Georgie's background. It was also decisive in inclining Borges towards the People of the Book.

---

[18] Borges probably alludes to these Bibles when he writes in "El libro de arena," which has autobiographical touches: "En esta casa hay algunas biblias inglesas, incluso la primera, la de Wiclif [sic]" (*El libro de arena*, p. 170).

[19] David Daiches, "The Influence of the Bible on English Literature" in *The Jews: Their History, Culture and Religion*, ed. Louis Finkelstein (Philadelphia: The Jewish Publication Society of America, 1966), II, 1469.

[20] Oded Sverdlik, "Borges habla de Israel y los judíos," *Nuevo mundo israelita* (Caracas), No. 190, 25 March–1 Apr. 1977, p. 3.

2. Jewish Friends, German Texts

The Trip-to-Europe has been a constant in Argentine life and letters.[1] Its basic purpose was to make contact with the centers of Western civilization, whether for utilitarian, esthetic or educational reasons. In the case of the Borgeses the motives were combined: Father would consult European specialists about his failing eyesight; Father and Mother would tour the cultural centers of the Continent; and Georgie and his sister, Norah, would go to school.

After traveling to London and Paris, the family settled in Geneva where they would remain until 1918. Jorge Luis was sent to the Collège Calvin. He recalls: "In my class there were some forty of us; a good half were foreigners."[2] Foreignness characterized not only the students. The linguistic codes of the school were likewise alien to the adolescent Argentine, since

[1] See on this David Viñas, "El viaje a Europa," in *Literatura argentina y realidad política: de Sarmiento a Cortázar* (Buenos Aires: Siglo Veinte, 1971).
[2] Jorge Luis Borges, "Autobiographical Essay," in *The Aleph and Other Stories 1933–1969*, ed. and trans. Norman Thomas di Giovanni in collaboration with the author (New York: Dutton, 1970), p. 214.

11

French was the language of study and Latin the chief subject of the curriculum. Georgie became proficient in both. He also made two close friends from among the foreigners, Simon Jichlinski and Maurice Abramowicz, Jews of Polish extraction. On innumerable occasions, when discussing his interest in Judaism, Borges has alluded to these schoolmates:

> Además de los libros . . . hay otro hecho. Es el hecho de mis amistades, de tantos amigos judíos. En Ginebra, ¿por qué no mencionar a Simon Jennisky y a Mauricio Abromovich [sic]?[3]

These were probably the first Jews with whom Borges had intimate, continued contact. Together, the trio experienced the varied landscape of teenage life; Abramowicz, who had poetic inclinations, introduced Jorge Luis to the works of Rimbaud and provided him with a sounding board on literary matters. Eventually, he helped Georgie publish in the Genevan paper, *La Feuille*.[4]

The friendship between Borges, Jichlinski and Abramowicz was lasting. After Jorge Luis left Switzerland they continued to correspond and in 1963—close to forty years later—Borges was reunited with his old school chums during a visit to Geneva. In his stories, Borges has scattered references to the two; it is another way of noting the fond memories of those Swiss days.[5]

---

[3] "Los primeros 25 años de *Davar*," p. 71. The spelling of the names Jichlinski and Abramowicz varies greatly in the various texts I consulted. During a personal interview I had with Borges on 6 Dec. 1979, he also spoke of these Jewish companions in Switzerland, noting: "The only two real friends I had were two Swiss citizens whose names, hardly Helvetic, were Simon Jichlinski and Maurice Abramowicz."

[4] See Emir Rodríguez Monegal, "Borges y la política," *Revista iberoamericana*, 43, Nos. 100–101 (1977), 273 and 290.

[5] Abramowicz is mentioned in "Tres versiones de Judas," *OC*, 516–17; and "Homenaje a César Paladión," *Crónicas de Bustos Domecq*, coauthored by Borges with Adolfo Bioy Casares (Buenos Aires: Losada, 1967), p. 17. Jichlinski appears in "El otro," *El libro de arena*, p. 19. M. Jichlinski, in a letter to me, also mentions the following reference to himself in Borges's work: "J'ai trouvé, il y a bien des années, avec une lettre qu'il m'adressait, une page d'une revue littéraire, portant le titre: 'Un poète lyrique autrichien d'aujourd'hui (en espagnol) *Simon Jichlinski*,' coiffant un poème dont j'aurais été bien incapable d'écrire le premier vers! Je lui avais alors demandé ce que cela signifiait, il m'a répondu qu'il avait publié ce poème comme la traduction d'un texte allemand,

Such warmth of feeling, coupled with possible ambiguities in some of Borges's statements about his relations with the Polish-Jewish pair (or misinterpretations of those statements), has given the impression that they were founts of Jewish knowledge, particularly kabbalistic, for their friend from Argentina. There is, for example, the following exchange between Borges and Ronald Christ during an interview:

> Interviewer: What about the Kabbalah? When did you first get interested in that?
>
> Borges: . . . When I lived in Geneva I had two personal, two great friends—Maurice Abramowicz and Seymour [sic] Jichlinski—their names tell you the stock they sprang from: they were Polish Jews.[6]

Borges does mention his Genevan Jewish schoolmates here in connection with a question on the Kabbalah. But he does *not* say that Abramowicz and Jichlinski revealed Jewish esoteric doctrine to him. Rather, he is apparently associating in his mind and in his answer two aspects of Judaism important to him: Jewish mysticism and Jewish friendship. "Kabbalah" and "Jichlinski-Abramowicz" are mentioned together because they come under the same heading: Judaism.

Simon Jichlinski confirms this interpretation. In a letter, he explains that during the years of his friendship with Borges, allusions to Judaism between them were rather rare,[7] but adds: "On peut tout au plus penser que, parce que nous étions juifs, l'esprit de Borges aurait pu, comme il était intéressé par tout, l'inciter à s'intéresser au judaïsme."[8] Though Borges has

---

se servant de mon nom car le style et le fond ne correspondaient pas à ce qu'il avait l'habitude de publier alors, comme chef de l'école ultraïste" (3 June 1979).

[6] Ronald Christ, "The Art of Fiction," *The Paris Review*, No. 40 (1967), p. 161. Borges likewise connected his Swiss Jewish friends and "Jewish sources" in a conversation with Y. Tirah, "J. L. Borges—On the 'Holy Spirit'," *Haaretz* (Tel Aviv), 24 Jan. 1969, p. 16. See also Marcos Ricardo Barnatán, "Una vindicación de la cábala," in *Conocer Borges y su obra* (Barcelona: Dopesa, 1978), p. 61.

[7] Letter from Simon Jichlinski, 19 May 1979. M. Abramowicz was too ill to respond to questions I sent him. In January, 1984, shortly after Abramowicz's death, Borges wrote a moving elegy to his friend, "Elegía," published in *La Nación*, 29 Jan. 1984, Sec. 2, p. 1.

[8] Letter, 3 June 1979. When I spoke to him, Borges confirmed what Jichlinski writes, saying that all the Jewish knowledge he gained from his

often pictured himself as a man shaped by books, whose writing is but a reelaboration of previous authors, the formative influence of people on him should not be underestimated. Given the positive mind set towards things Jewish that was Georgie's inheritance, the camaraderie with two Jews, contemporaries in age and in inclinations, and like him strangers in a foreign land (Borges always emphasizes the standoffishness of the Swiss towards outsiders), could not have but struck a responsive chord.

Borges traces the beginnings of his interest in Judaism precisely to the Swiss years: "Since my Genevan days, I had always been interested in Jewish culture" ("Autobiographical Essay," p. 257). In Switzerland he found the gift of Jewish friendship; but he also discovered Jewish culture, the poetry, folklore and mysticism created by Jews. These two aspects of Judaism may have been related in a subliminal way, as Jichlinski theorizes. The direct, documented agent of Borges's initiation into Jewish culture was, however, a language and its texts:

> Luego vinieron aquellos años de la primera guerra mundial y fue . . . mi estudio del alemán lo que me llevó a lo hebreo . . . Yo entré en el idioma alemán apenas desflorado por la poesía de Heine y por la prosa de Gustavo Meyrink.
>
> ("Los primeros 25 años de *Davar*," p. 71)

English had been the linguistic code which opened up the world of Scripture; through French, Borges gained his Jewish friends; now German uncovered a new layer of Jewish experience.

Borges has recounted how he came to German. After being "dazzled and also bewildered" by a reading of Carlyle's *Sartor Resartus*—whose hero, Diogenes Teufelsdroeckh, is a German professor of idealism—Borges decided to take up the "language of the philosophers" ("Autobiographical Essay," p. 216). He plunged into the *Critique of Pure Reason*, but the Kantian prose "defeated" him and he turned instead to

---

friends consisted of some chance words in Hebrew, but that their being Jewish "must have been" influential in the formation of his interest in Judaism.

poetry, choosing Heine's *Lyrisches Intermezzo*. The simple vocabulary allowed Georgie to work his way into "the loveliness of the language" and before long he read it well enough to tackle a bestseller of the moment, Gustav Meyrink's *Der Golem* (1915). This phantasy of the Prague ghetto was the first German book Borges read from cover to cover.

It is worthwhile to pause and examine the episode of Borges's coming to the Jewish via the German. The facts are illustrative first, of the way Borges has gained most of his knowledge of Judaism, and second, of his definition of Jewishness. According to the author, just as the reading of an English work brought him to German culture so did the study of German writings bring him to Jewish culture. But to become familiar with the heritage of Germany (the message), Borges mastered the medium (German). That did not happen in the second case. Borges never learned Hebrew, nor Aramaic, the language of the Talmud and the *Zohar*, nor Yiddish, the vernacular of the Hassidic masters. His familiarity with those important portions of Jewish civilization not housed in the major European languages is secondary, gained from translations, reelaborations. Hebrew, Aramaic and Yiddish, written in a non-Latin script, were perhaps too forbidding for Borges; more likely, he felt no pressing need to know them. Borges approached Judaism as a creative writer, not as a professor of Semitics. If the Jewish material he required for his purposes was available in a form already accessible, there was no urgency to acquire the original linguistic codes. Also, since so much of Judaic civilization—Scripture, later books by Jews— has become intertwined and identified with the Western tradition (certainly in Borges's mind), the trio of tongues was not perceived as an indispensible tool. Judaism was Europe's birthright; it could be reached via European languages.

Borges had said that the study of German led him to *lo hebreo*. What does he include under that heading? Poetry without specific Jewish content by a German born into Judaism but converted to Christianity, and prose by a non-Jew based on a Judaic motif (the golem), but not centrally concerned with its Jewish meaning. Both works, nonetheless, are unequivocally identified as part of *lo hebreo*. Borges's conception of Jewish civilization is broad: any link, any association with Judaism is usually enough to place an author and a work within the "Hebrew" camp. Others may question Heine's Jewishness, or criticize the inadequacy of Meyrink's grasp of Jewish esoteric literature,[9] not Borges. For him, Heine is emblematic of the painful Jewish condition ("París, 1856," *OC*, 914), and *Der Golem*, a reflection of the ghetto, called by Borges "the magic greenhouse of Jewish culture."[10] A number of plausible explanations for this spacious view of *lo hebreo* come to mind. Borges himself (like Heine) is the product of a heterodox religious milieu; he is a non-Jew who (like Meyrink) cultivates Jewish themes in his art, but only negligibly, if at all, in his belief; and, as already has been pointed out, he approaches Judaism through the European tongues, the medium often used by more assimilated Jewish writers (Heine) and, of course, by non-Jews (Meyrink).

The entry into the Hebraic by means of the German which occurred in Switzerland was seminal in shaping the Jewish presence in Borges. Starting with the *Lyrisches Intermezzo* and *Der Golem*, German became a primary Jewish code for him. In German, Borges read studies on the Kabbalah, writings by Martin Buber and Fritz Mauthner, stories and novels by Franz Kafka, books by Max Brod and Lion Feuchtwanger, and poetry by the Expressionists Albert Ehrenstein, Franz Werfel, Alfred Doeblin and others.[11] Some of these texts

---

[9] See, for example, Jeffrey L. Sammons, *Heinrich Heine, The Elusive Poet* (New Haven and London: Yale University Press, 1969) in which the author, in a special appendix, argues against Heine's Jewishness. As for Meyrink, none other than Gershom Scholem, the illustrious authority on the Kabbalah, calls his Jewish sources in *Der Golem* "mauvaises sources" (Reported by Mircea Eliade, "Jugements contemporains: Mircea Eliade," in *Gustav Meyrink* [Paris: L'Herne, 1976], p. 234).

[10] Jorge Luis Borges, "Les Serres magiques de la culture juive," in *Gustav Meyrink*, pp. 106–107. The French text is a partial translation of Borges's prologue to *El Cardenal Napellus* (Buenos Aires: Librería La Ciudad/F. M. Ricci, 1979), a volume of Meyrink's stories translated into Spanish by María Esther Vázquez.

[11] The German books alluded to and the places they are mentioned follow: Erich Bischoff, *Die Elemente der Kabbalah* (Berlin, 1920)—"Historia de los

had recognizable Jewish content; others did not. Still all were examples of *lo hebreo*. The impact of the German Expressionists was particularly important in Borges's literary formation. The Expressionists' magical-metaphysical vision, and their ability to capture in literature the horror and chaos of the times, left durable marks on the future author, whose stories, some two decades later, would in many ways echo this vision and these concerns.

Borges had left Argentina as a fifteen-year-old little exposed to the outside world. In the years he spent in Switzerland (1914-1919), his circle of affection was enlarged to include two unforgettable friends, and his two original languages were expanded to five. Both acquisitions served as spurs for the development of positive links to Judaism. Borges's Swiss experience, building on the childhood liberal/extraterritorial foundation, added new dimensions to his understanding of *lo hebreo*. The next phase in his journey towards manly and literary maturity would be a potent sequel.

ángeles," *El tamaño de mi esperanza* (Buenos Aires: Proa, 1926), p. 67; Martin Buber, *Was ist der Mensch?* (1938) and *Gog und Magog* (1941)—"Historia de los ecos de un nombre," *OC*, 751; Fritz Mauthner, *Woerterbuch der Philosophie* (Munich, 1910)—"Entretiens avec James E. Irby," in *Jorge Luis Borges* (L'Herne: Paris, 1964), p. 400; Franz Kafka—most of "la obra extraordinaria," as Borges characterizes it, in "Libros y autores extranjeros," *El Hogar*, 29 Oct. 1937, p. 28, one of the innumerable times Borges speaks of Kafka; Max Brod, *Franz Kafka: Eine Biographie* (Prague, 1937)—"Libros y autores extranjeros," *El Hogar*, 8 July 1938, p. 28; Lion Feuchtwanger, *Jud Suess* (Munich, 1925)—"Libros y autores extranjeros," *El Hogar*, 13 Nov. 1936, p. 120; German Expressionists—Albert Ehrenstein in "Libros y autores extranjeros," *El Hogar*, 17 Sept. 1937, p. 24. Franz Werfel is mentioned there and, more extensively in "Libros y autores extranjeros," 16 April 1937, p. 28. Ehrenstein, Werfel and Alfred Doeblin are also recalled in "Letras alemanas: una exposición afligente," *Sur*, 8 No. 49 (Oct. 1938), 66.

17

3. Ultraism and Judaism

1919: the Borgeses leave Switzerland for Spain, intended as a stopover on the way back to Argentina. Majorca is the first place they visit; Seville follows; by 1920, the family is in Madrid where, in Borges's words, "the great event to me was my friendship with Rafael Cansinos-Asséns" ("Autobiographical Essay," p. 221).

An almost forgotten figure today, in the years following the Great War Cansinos-Asséns served as guru to a literary generation anxious to throw off the shackles of the old and embrace the ultramodern. This guiding impulse—a result in part of the horror of the World War I experience—was summed up in the word *ultraísmo*, under whose banner the poets of Seville and Madrid sought to adapt the innovations of the European avant-garde—Dadaism, Cubism, Surrealism, Expressionism—into Spanish.

Georgie, whose knowledge of German had already given him firsthand acquaintance with the work of the Expressionists (he was one of their early translators into Spanish), found in the Ultraists his kind of people, poets, men whose profession was literature and whose endless hours in the cafés were spent discussing such topics as The Metaphor and Traditional Forms of Poetry ("Autobiographical Essay," p. 221). It was on the pages of their journals that he published his early poems and articles.

The Ultraist leader, Cansinos-Asséns, was a particular revelation. Here was a colorful and brilliant man of letters, versed in a myriad of languages, including Hebrew and Arabic, a translator of authors as diverse as De Quincey, Pirandello, and Dostoyevsky, and the creator of essays, poems, stories and novels. The young Argentine was so magnetized by this intellect, that he became an active participant in the weekly literary salon over which Cansinos presided at Madrid's Café Colonial.[1] Decades later, Borges could still say without hesitation that he considered himself Cansinos's disciple.[2]

Such devotion to an author whose writings are generally little-remembered has puzzled as perceptive a student of Borges's *oeuvre* as Emir Rodríguez Monegal.[3] Speaking of Cansinos's impact on the Argentine, the Uruguayan critic notes it ''was so great that he . . . acknowledged him as his master —a view that now seems hard to share'' (*Biography*, p. 161).

The difficulty in agreeing with Borges hinges on the understanding of the word ''master.'' In what sense is Cansinos the master and Borges the disciple? Certainly not in literary skill and novelty: Borges is by far the superior writer, the master. But this is only one aspect of the matter. To get at the meaning *Borges* gives to the laudatory epithet, his own words must serve as guide:

Cansinos seems to me . . . like the symbol of all culture, Western and Eastern. . . . I was stimulated by him to far-flung reading. In writing, I began aping him. He wrote long and flowing sentences with an un-Spanish and strongly Hebrew flavor to them. (''Autobiographical Essay,'' pp. 221–22)

---

[1] Borges recalls those days in ''La traducción de un incidente,'' *Inquisiciones* (Buenos Aires: Proa, 1925), pp. 15–19.

[2] Jorge Luis Borges, ''Homenaje a Rafael Cansinos-Asséns,'' *Davar*, No. 101 (1964), p. 8.

[3] I am referring to general histories of literature. More specific works on the period, for example, Gloria Videla, *El ultraísmo* (Madrid: Gredos, 1963), speak of Cansinos.

What this statement suggests is that Borges saw in Cansinos a role model, a mentor and a teacher who buttressed and extended tendencies already present in the future author of *El Aleph*. Chief among them were the interrelated cosmopolitanism—the interest in foreign cultures, other languages, distant places, bygone eras—and Hebraism.

Cansinos advocated both, placing himself at opposite poles from the nationalistic, Catholic writers and critics of his period. In a novel about the Ultraist adventure, *El movimiento V.P.*, he makes clear his position in the ongoing battle between the two Spains, one traditionalist, orthodox and usually anti-Semitic, the other liberal, heterodox and more sympathetic to Judaism:

> ¡Verdaderamente que estos Poetas de la Raza y estos Críticos de la Raza me han inspirado siempre una repugnancia invencible! . . . Yo quiero ser un poeta de todas las razas: de la raza blanca, de la raza amarilla, de la raza negra, y hasta de la raza canina . . . ¡Oh estrellas que me miráis, y a las que podría saludar en veinte idiomas clásicos y vulgares, vosotras sois testigos de mi perfecto desinterés en cuanto a la raza! . . . Yo tengo el don de las lenguas como prenda de una estirpe nómada y cosmopolita; . . . yo amo igualmente la sinagoga en que se custodia un libro antiguo y la Catedral donde se exhibe en viriles de oro el sol de cada día.[4]

His adversaries understand and attack this attitude in no uncertain terms, execrating their most terrible enemy, the exotic, heretical, antinationalist poet in whose ancestry, they claim, there are surely traces of Moorish and Jewish blood (p. 220).

For Cansinos—as earlier for Father Borges—Judaism was definitely part of an anti-Establishment posture: to do away with traditional thinking, with canonical forms of art. But the label "Jewish" was more than a catchword indicating anything innovative, rebellious or cosmopolitan. As his works reveal, Cansinos had a deep, direct knowledge of Judaic sources and a strong attachment to the Jewish people. He was one of the pioneers of the Judeo-Spanish rapprochement of the twentieth century and a precursor of the "Judaizing" trend in

---

[4] Rafael Cansinos-Asséns, *El movimiento V.P.* (Madrid: Mundo Latino, 1921), pp. 101–03.

Spanish literary criticism whose most famous exponent was Américo Castro. In 1920, for example, while Borges was in Spain, Cansinos published two important books of exclusively Judaic content: the collection of articles and essays, *España y los judíos españoles*, which described his work in support of the Jewish people and suggested Judaic elements in Cervantes's work (a topic later developed by Castro); and *Las bellezas del Talmud*, probably the first translation of Talmudic lore into Spanish.[5] His disciple, Borges, was fully aware of this philo-Semitism:

> [Cansinos] had come from Seville, where he had studied for the priesthood, but, having found the name Cansinos in the archives of the Inquisition, he decided he was a Jew. This led him to the study of Hebrew, and later on he even had himself circumcised. ("Autobiographical Essay," p. 221)

He was also entirely cognizant of the link between Cansinos's cosmopolitanism and his Hebraism: "Cansinos es judeo-español. Ese conocerse judío lo universaliza, lo extraña de lo provinciano europeo, lo suelta como un viaje—ese viaje que nunca hizo."[6]

Living in Spain at the time when Cansinos was carrying out many of his activities on behalf of the Jewish cause, sharing with the Master sessions at the café and after-dark walks spent in conversation, visiting Cansinos's infinite library, getting to know the Andalusian's creative and critical writings with their heavy dose of Hebraism,[7] Borges came to understand, absorb and express the essence of the man:

---

[5] Rafael Cansinos-Asséns, *España y los judíos españoles* (Tortosa: Monclús, 1920); and *Las bellezas del Talmud* (Madrid: América, 1920).

[6] "Bibliografía y notas," *Síntesis* (Buenos Aires), 1, No. 1 (June, 1927), 110.

[7] On Cansinos's pro-Jewish activities of the time, see *España y los judíos españoles*. Borges's poem, "A Rafael Cansinos-Asséns" in *Luna de enfrente* (1925) included in *Poemas, 1922–43* (Buenos Aires: Losada, 1943), pp. 95–6, describes their walks. In the "Autobiographical Essay," Borges recalls a visit to Cansinos's library (p. 222); and in "La creación y P. H. Gosse" (*OC*, 652) and "Homenaje a Cansinos-Asséns" (p. 8), he mentions his favorites among the guru's books: *Las bellezas del Talmud; Psalmos. El candelabro de los siete brazos* (1914), a volume of prose poems in Cansinos's Hebraically-inspired style; and

La imagen de aquel pueblo lapidado
Y execrado, inmortal en su agonía,
En las negras vigilias lo atraía
Con una suerte de terror sagrado.
Bebió como quien bebe un hondo vino
Los Psalmos y el Cantar de la Escritura
Y sintió que era suya esa dulzura
Y sintió que era suyo aquel destino,
Lo llamaba Israel.

("Rafael Cansinos-Asséns," *OC*, 915)

Humanly and literarily Borges grew to "ape" Cansinos (to use his own term). From a novice poet who imitated the guru's "sentences with an un-Spanish and strongly Hebrew flavor," to the mature narrator moved by "that lapidated folk" and its heritage, to the septuagenarian man of letters who says, "I have done everything possible to be Jewish" (Guibert, p. 353), Borges has paid tribute to this master, the person to a great extent responsible for his laudatory approach to Judaism.[8]

With the impressions of Spain and Cansinos fresh in his mind, Jorge Luis returned to Buenos Aires in 1921. The homecoming, after an absence of seven eventful years, marked the beginning of a search for a personal formula to integrate the lessons learned in Europe with Argentine reality. In this process the Jew—now a part of Argentine society—provided additional dimensions to what was to become the Jewish presence in Borges.

Los temas literarios y su interpretación (1924), a collection of critical essays, some on Jewish topics.

[8] I discuss Cansinos's Jewish influence on Borges further in my article, "Cansinos-Asséns y Borges: en busca del vínculo judaico," *Revista iberoamericana*, 46, Nos. 112–113 (1980), 533–44.

4. The Jewry Is on Talcahuano and Libertad

Until the time of his return home, Argentine reality and Argentine letters contributed little to Borges's interest in Judaism. During his childhood, (1899–1914), Jewish life in the River Plate republic was as yet in its early stages. The large-scale immigration that would make the Argentine Jewish community one of the most important in the world did not begin till the late 1880's,[1] so it is not surprising that Borges makes no mention of contact with Jews prior to his European years. This lack of contact with Argentine Jews is matched by an absence of references to Argentine books by or on Jews—with an exception soon to be discussed. In Switzerland, Georgie met not only Abramowicz and Jichlinski; he also came to know of Heine and Meyrink. Nothing comparable occurred in pre-Great War Buenos Aires.

The explanation is hardly esoteric. At that time, the Jewish intelligentsia which has contributed so greatly to Ar-

---

[1] For the history of the Argentine Jewish community, see Alberto Klein, *Cinco siglos de historia: una crónica de la vida judía en la Argentina* (Buenos Aires: Comité Judío Americano, 1976); and Robert Weisbrot, *The Jews of Argentina: from the Inquisition to Perón* (Philadelphia: Jewish Publication Society of America, 1979).

gentina's cultural life was just beginning its activity.[2] 1910, the date of the centennial of Argentina's independence, marked the appearance of the first literary work written in Spanish by an Argentine Jew: Alberto Gerchunoff's *Los gauchos judíos*. The collection of short stories based on the writer's experiences in the Jewish farming villages of the pampa, became a classic of (Judeo-)Argentine letters partly because it was a pioneering effort, a watershed. (Borges was later to know it, comment upon it and utilize it in his fictions.[3]) Only in the 1920's and '30's—when Jews were more numerous and more comfortable in Argentina's society—did the community produce writers like César Tiempo, Carlos M. Grünberg, Samuel Eichelbaum and Bernardo Verbitsky.

But if at the start of the century the Jew was still absent from Argentine letters as creator, he was already present as subject. Non-Jewish writers, reacting to the massive immigration which was changing the face of Argentina, saw in the Jew, along with other newcomers, a symbol of all they considered wrong with the country.[4] One of the literary successes of the period was *La bolsa* (1891), by Julián Martel, an anti-Semitic novel full of diatribes against the "descendents of Judas," allegedly out to conquer America with an army of Jewish bankers and usurers.[5] So popular was this work, that it was quite likely the only Argentine book dealing with Jews to be read by Georgie before the Genevan days (Vázquez, *Borges*, p.

---

[2] On the place and image of Jews in Argentine literature, see Kessel Schwartz, "The Jew in Twentieth-Century Argentine Fiction," *The American Hispanist*, 3 (Sept. 1977), 9–12; and Robert Goodman, "The Image of the Jew in Argentine Literature as Seen by Argentine Jewish Writers," Diss. New York University, 1972.

[3] See Borges's "El indigno," *OC*, 1029–33; and "La forma de la gloria," in Jorge Luis Borges and Adolfo Bioy Casares, *Nuevos cuentos de Bustos Domecq* (Buenos Aires: Librería La Ciudad, 1977), pp. 117–28. This subject will be discussed in detail in the second part of my study.

[4] German García, *El inmigrante en la novela argentina* (Buenos Aires: Hachette, 1970); and Gladys S. Onega, *La inmigración en la literatura argentina, 1880–1910* (Santa Fe: Universidad del Litoral, 1965) deal with this topic.

[5] I have consulted the 1956 edition of *La bolsa* (Buenos Aires: Kraft). For a study on the anti-Semitism in the novel, consult David Viñas in "Martel y los culpables del 90," *Oligarquía*, pp. 71–93.

36). As such, the work may be an Argentine source—along with the more famous Shylock and other myths—for the only avaricious Jew in Borges's work: Aarón Loewenthal of "Emma Zunz."[6] (The story, like *La bolsa*, has an Argentine setting.) The xenophobia that Martel gave voice to in *La bolsa* was the extreme edge of a nationalism that gathered strength in Argentina from the end of the century, in some cases eventually coalescing with fascist philosophies coming out of Europe. More and more, the cosmopolitanism which had been an important strain in the thinking of Argentina's Europeanizing nation builders—and an essential ingredient in Borges's formation—was tempered by a reevaluation of native values. Even the vanguardist writers of the post-World War I era, like their European cousins imbued with an enthusiastic internationalism, took part in the turning homeward.[7]

When Borges came back to his land of birth, the mood of the moment coincided with his personal circumstance: the need to take hold of the indigenous landscape after so many wanderings. The result was a period of nativism in which Borges sought to reidentify with his Argentine heritage by becoming the keen observer and singer of the traditional Buenos Aires of his childhood, the big town fast disappearing under the influence of immigration and modern development. His first books of poems and essays, from *Fervor de Buenos Aires* (1923) to *Evaristo Carriego* (1930), all reflect this localist tone, as Borges took note of a common complaint of the time: Our republic is being overrun by foreigners; we are losing it.[8] If there was any moment in his development when Borges may have retreated into a less friendly attitude towards Judaism, this might have been it. But the weight of his universalist formation, coupled with the reality of the new Jewish presence in Buenos Aires, served as a counterbalance.

---

[6] See the chapters, "A Vindication of the Kabbalah" and "A Man Who Is the Book, . . . the Jew," in this study.

[7] Marta Scrimaglio in *Literatura argentina de vanguardia: 1920–30* (Rosario: Biblioteca, 1974) analyzes the turning homeward of the vanguardist writers.

[8] "Queja de todo criollo," *Inquisiciones*, p. 138.

In his books Borges advocates nativism, yes; but it must be, as he describes it, a cosmopolitan nativism which is open to other cultural currents and to his own metaphysical-religious interests—both categories that include Judaism.[9] The very same books of the 1920–30 decade, cited over and again for their domesticity, contain multiple examples of *lo hebreo*: references to the Bible, the Kabbalah and the seven-branched candelabrum as well as allusions to the Jews in Spain, the Jewishness of German Expressionism and the Wandering Jew.[10] At the same time, Borges's nostalgic recreation of the Buenos Aires of yesteryear does not preclude his appreciation of the changed city, the cosmopolitan Babel in which Jews are a noticeable component. Thus he writes soon after his return home: "En este mi Buenos Aires, lo babélico, lo pintoresco, lo desgajado de las cuatro puntas del mundo, es decoro del Centro. La morería esta en Reconquista y la judería en Talcahuano y Libertad."[11] This Jewish presence in Buenos Aires, and elsewhere in Argentina, would not only help Borges retain and strengthen his ties with Judaism; it would also provide him with material for his stories—"Emma Zunz," "El indigno," "Guayaquil"—and other writings.

Throughout the 1920's Borges began to build his contacts with the Argentine Jewish community, particularly with its intellectuals. He participated in literary gatherings and shared the pages of important journals—*Proa* and *Martín Fierro*—with writers like Tiempo, Gerchunoff and Grünberg, men whose work he came to know and with whom he frequently developed cordial relationships.[12] In addition, as of 1928, he pub-

[9] "El tamaño de mi esperanza," *El tamaño de mi esperanza* (Buenos Aires: Proa, 1926), p. 10.

[10] Some of these references are: (a) the Bible—mentioned innumerable times, for example in "Examen de metáforas," *Inquisiciones*, p. 69; (b) the Kabbalah—"Historia de los ángeles," *El tamaño de mi esperanza*, pp. 67–68; (c) Seven-branched candelabrum—"Dualidá en una despedida," *Luna de enfrente*, *Poemas*, p. 86; (d) Jews in Spain—"Las luminarias de Hanukah," *El tamaño de mi esperanza*, p. 95; (e) German Expressionism—"Acerca del expresionismo," *Inquisiciones*, pp. 146–152; (f) Wandering Jew—"Saint Joan, a Chronicle Play," *El tamaño de mi esperanza*, p. 101.

[11] "La pampa y el suburbio son dioses," *El tamaño de mi esperanza*, p. 22.

[12] See on *Proa* and *Martín Fierro*, David Oberstar, "An Analysis of *Proa* (1924–26): Vanguard Literary Journal of the Argentine," Diss. University of

lished several of his books under the imprint of Manuel Gleizer, a pioneer of the literary publishing business in Argentina together with several other Jewish immigrants.[13] This Jewish editor of Borges's found his way into a half-serious, half-joking piece written by the author in 1934. Entitled "Yo, judío," the article was a caustic retort to comments made in the right-wing magazine *Crisol* about Borges's alleged "Jewish ancestry, maliciously hidden" (p. 60).[14] Poking fun at the anti-Semites' attempt to smear him by discovering Jewish blood in his veins, Borges openly admits that his maternal surname, Acevedo, was probably borne by Portuguese Jews reaching the River Plate region in colonial times. To have such Jewish ancestry would not bother him in the least, Borges notes—indeed it would please him—but (alas!) geneological research has shown that *his* colonial ancestor was one Don Pedro de Azevedo, a Spaniard from Catalonia (p. 60).[15] Concludes the author with tongue-firmly-in-cheek:

Agradezco el estímulo de *Crisol*, pero está enflaqueciendo mi esperanza de entroncar con la Mesa de los Panes y con el Mar de Bronce, con Heine, Gleizer y las diez Sefiroth, con el Eclesiastés y con Chaplin. (p. 60)

The enumeration (a favorite stylistic device in Borges) is a

Kansas, 1973; and Adolfo Prieto, *El periódico "Martín Fierro"* (Buenos Aires: Galerna, 1968). César Tiempo recalled Borges's contacts with him and other Judeo-Argentine intellectuals in an interview I had with him (12 Aug. 1980). He noted that Borges had always been "close to the Jewish community." Consult also, César Tiempo, "Diálogo con Cansinos Asséns," *Davar*, No. 85 (1960), p. 21. On Borges's acquaintance with Gerchunoff and his work, see his prologue to Gerchunoff's *Retorno a Don Quijote* (Buenos Aires: Sudamericana, 1951). Borges became particularly friendly with Grünberg, as indicated in Jorge Luis Borges, "Homenaje a Carlos Grünberg," *Davar*, No. 119 (1968), pp. 28–29.

[13] Consult "Editores judíos de libros argentinos," *Comentario* (Buenos Aires), No. 38 (1964), pp. 64–71. Borges published *El idioma de los argentinos* (1928), *Evaristo Carriego* (1930) and *Discusión* (1932) with Gleizer.

[14] Jorge Luis Borges, "Yo, judío," *Megáfono*, 3, No. 12 (Apr. 1934), 60.

[15] The fact that one of his family names was also used by Jews has intrigued Borges. Though it does not form the essence of his interest in Judaism, which is a result of the factors I have been tracing, he has cited it as one more reason for his fascination with things Jewish.

catalogue of things he associates with Judaism: Scripture, biblical miracles, the author of the *Lyrisches Intermezzo*, the great silent-film comic and Manuel Gleizer. While obviously humorous, the list does touch some fundamental notes in Borges's Jewish keyboard. The inclusion of Gleizer, perhaps in the writer's mind as a result of their dealings, is a nod of acknowledgement to Argentine Jewry, which was beginning to play a role in the Jewish theme in Borges.

"Yo, judío" divulges more than its author's Judaic preferences or his recognition of Manuel Gleizer, however. The fact that the article appeared in the first place is an indication of the winds blowing in Argentina as the twenties closed and the thirties began. In 1924, Leopoldo Lugones, with his sensitive, if misguided poet's antennae, gave expression to the mood of the moment in a now-famous speech in which he announced the Hour of the Sword: the time that would put to an end the bankrupt evils of pacifism, collectivism and democracy and offer Argentina the rule of a military strongman, with or without law.[16] It was a call for an Argentine rendition of the socio-political tunes played in France by the reactionary neo-monarchist Charles Maurras and in Italy by the triumphant fascist Benito Mussolini. (Later, Germany's Adolph Hitler would also be a model for emulation.) This shift to the right was an attempt by the old-line Hispano-Creole oligarchy to turn the clock back to preimmigration Argentina when hierarchy, discipline and law-and-order were the watchwords, rather than universal suffrage, economic emancipation and social justice. Such a philosophy was inevitably riddled with xenophobia, of which anti-Semitism was a significant subheading.

Borges, writing at about the same time, had taken note of the "foreignization" of Argentina. But *his* nativism served as a strategy for readaptation to Buenos Aires and as a poetic formula—not as a gateway to fascism. His nonadherence to the ultranationalist cause was undoubtedly one reason for the

---

[16] Lugones's speech is quoted by Luis C. Alén Lascano in *La Argentina ilusionada* (Buenos Aires: La Bastilla, 1975), p. 145.

anti-Semitic *Crisol* article: those whose clock did not mark the Hour of the Sword could only be Jews or Jew-lovers. Until this period, Borges's Judaism had been largely fueled by positive forces. Now a negative force, anti-Semitism, was to become an important stimulus.The era of the writer's major production, of those works on which his reputation rests, was also the period of the Second World War, during which the hell Nazism created served to bring Borges closer to the people he called "that execrated folk."

5. Nazism and Judaism

In 1930 General José F. Uriburu overthrew the tottering Irigoyen regime; Lugones's Hour of the Sword received legitimacy as Argentina's form of government. The period following the coup—called the "infamous decade" although it lasted until 1943—saw the intensification of ultranationalism and anti-Semitism spurred by a conservative crusade to free the fatherland of the "evils" of democracy and cosmopolitanism.[1] Developments in Europe strengthened the nationalists' hand. The Nazi persecution of the Jews served as an incentive to local racists seeking a solution to Argentina's own "Jewish problem." One of their most visible representatives, Gustavo Adolfo Martínez Zuviría, Director of the National Library (a position later held by Borges), practically called for their extermination in his two volume anti-Semitic novel, *El Kahal, Oro* (1935) where he equated patriotism with Jew-hatred, claiming that the cry "Death to the Jews" is almost synony-

---

[1] José Luis Romero in *A History of Argentine Political Thought*, introd. and trans. Thomas F. McGann (Stanford: Stanford University Press, 1963), discusses the "infamous decade" under the heading "The Course of Fascism," pp. 227–56.

mous with "Long Live the Fatherland."[2] As Europe moved towards and into war, pro-Nazi sentiments in Argentina were fanned by German agents, some Argentines of German descent and other fascist sympathizers. In 1938, the Comité contra el Racismo y el Antisemitismo en la Argentina—formed by distinguished Jewish and non-Jewish personalities—saw fit to issue the following warning:

Si queremos evitar que el problema racial—y concretamente el antisemitismo—adquiera entre nosotros la misma monstruosa significación que en los países totalitarios, debemos exponerlo al pueblo con toda claridad . . . Ninguna tradición puede preservarnos contra la inflitración nazi-fascista—uno de cuyos aspectos es el racismo—, inflitración que entre nosotros ha adquirido una importancia insospechable.[3]

One of the prominent Argentines who supported this call to fight anti-Semitism was none other than Jorge Luis Borges who appears in the Comité's records as an advisor and as a member of the organizing commission for the First Congress against Racism and Anti-Semitism held in Buenos Aires on August 6th and 7th, 1938.[4]

The proceedings of the Congress do not reveal any formal participation by Borges. Although the writer felt strongly enough about the committee's aims to join it, the mass meetings and fiery speeches, which were an essential part of the organization's program, were not his style.[5] He was opposed to anti-Semitism, but he would have to find other platforms to attack it. And find them he did.

---

[2] Quoted in Juan José Sebreli, *La cuestión judía en la Argentina* (Buenos Aires: Tiempo Contemporáneo, 1968), p. 134.

[3] *Actas del Primer Congreso contra el Racismo y el Antisemitismo* (Buenos Aires: Comité contra el Racismo y el Antisemitismo en la Argentina, 1938), "palabras preliminares."

[4] This information is culled from the *Actas*.

[5] One mass meeting on record, aside from the August 6–7 congress, was held on 19 April 1938 at the Casa Suiza. See, *El pueblo contra la invasión nazi* (Buenos Aires: Comité contra el Racismo y el Antisemitismo en la Argentina, 1938), a pamphlet which contains the texts of the speeches given on that occasion. Borges is again listed as an advisor of the Comité. On Borges's unease at social gatherings and aversion to speaking in public see, *Biography*, pp. 298–99. The author only overcame these inhibitions in later years.

The articles Borges published in the thirties and forties became his podium, his weapon in a campaign to denounce Nazism and its persecution of the Jews. Borges was genuinely outraged by what was happening in Europe and equally piqued by the reverberations in Argentina. This is evident from reading his contributions to *Sur* and *El Hogar*, the two magazines whose pages are the primary record of Borges's anti-fascist polemic.

Sur, an influential cultural journal to whose inner circle Borges belonged from the outset, had been founded in 1931 by Victoria Ocampo. One of those instrumental in persuading the aristocratic, idiosyncratic Victoria to launch the publication was the American-Jewish writer, Waldo Frank, a recent visitor to Argentina. Frank had been born into a family little connected to its ancestral faith, but in 1920 underwent a mystical reconversion to Judaism and after that put things Jewish on his human and literary agenda. During the 1930's and '40's he contributed several moving articles to *Sur* in which he decried Nazi policies, reaffirmed his own Jewishness and expressed his thoughts on the Jewish contribution to America.[6]

What influence Frank had on *Sur*'s position vis-à-vis fascist anti-Semitism is hard to determine; nonetheless, the journal clearly stated its position in an editorial:

> Todas las persecuciones sectarias—sean de raza, sean de política, sean injustas persecuciones disimuladas bajo formas codificadas y legales—nos parecen igualmente odiosas, igualmente monstruosas.
>
> (7, No. 35, Aug. 1937, 8)

It was a stand enunciated by Victoria Ocampo and maintained throughout the World War II years, a period in which *Sur* resounded with the echoes of the conflict and of the Nazi campaign to exterminate the Jews. Thus, in 1938, *Sur* published under its imprint *Los judíos entre las naciones* by Jacques

---

[6] The first issue of *Sur*, 1, No. 1 (Summer 1931), 7–18, opens with a "Carta a Waldo Frank" by Victoria Ocampo in which she tells the story of Frank's part in inspiring the journal. Frank's articles on world Jewry during the Hitler era are "¿Por qué ha de sobrevivir el judío?" 4, No. 9 (May 1934), 152–70; and "El judío en el futuro de América," 10, No. 77 (Feb. 1941), 12–20.

Maritain, a French-Catholic philosopher who was an outspoken champion of the Jewish cause during the Nazi period (reported in 8, No. 46, July 1938, n. pag.) As the Continent moved closer to war, *Sur* reported on the sufferings of German Jews in concentration camps (9, No. 53, Feb. 1939, 84–85) and reiterated its stand against all dictatorship and oppression (9, No. 60, Sept. 1939, 7–9). Issues of the journal were dedicated to the outbreak of the war (9, No. 61, Oct. 1939), to the liberation of France (14, No. 120, Oct. 1944) and to the peace which ended the hostilities (15, No. 140, June 1946). Always, the emphasis, signaled by the Anglo- and Francophile Ocampo was prodemocratic and antifascist. When the magnitude of the Holocaust became known, *Sur* featured essays like Giuliana Tedeschi's "Recuerdos de Auschwitz" (15, No. 140, June 1946, 44–60) and Jean Paul Sartre's "Retrato del antisemita" (15, No. 138, Apr. 1946, 7–41).

Borges's contributions to *Sur* in the war era should be seen in the light of this orientation, because the writer was a chief exponent of the journal's antifascist position. Through his articles, from "Una pedagogía del odio," blasting Nazi anti-Semitic literature (1937), to "Nota sobre la paz," a paean to England's victory over Germany (1945), Borges gave voice to *Sur*'s policy of indignation in the face of the Hitlerite excesses. [7] At the same time, Borges the creative writer used to good advantage the stance espoused by the review. Between 1939 and 1946 *Sur* became the platform from which Borges launched many of his now-famous fictions. On its pages readers were first introduced to the innovative narrations

---

[7] Borges's *Sur* articles on the subjects of fascism and anti-Semitism between 1937 and 1945 are:
—"Letras alemanas: una pedagogía del odio," 7, No. 32 (May 1937), 80–81.
—"Letras alemanas: una exposición afligente" 8, No. 49 (Oct. 1938), 66–67.
—"Ensayo de imparcialidad," 9, No. 61 (Oct. 1939), 27–29.
—"1941," 12, No. 87 (Dec. 1941), 21–22.
—"Anotación al 23 de agosto de 1944," 14, No. 120 (Oct. 1944), 24–25.
—"Nota sobre la paz," 14, No. 129 (July 1945), 9–10. Borges's review of Gilbert Waterhouse's *A Short History of German Literature* (London, 1943), 12, No. 104 (May–June 1943), 86–7, while not directly on the subject, alludes to it.

which gave Borges the epithet of master mythmaker.[8] In these stories—"Tlön, Uqbar, Orbis Tertius" (1940), "El milagro secreto" (1943) and "Deutsches Requiem" (1946) are good examples—totalitarianism, Nazism, anti-Semitism are considered abominations. Jewish culture, the object of the Teutonic onslaught, is accorded a prominent place. (See "La muerte y la brújula" [1942] or "El Aleph" [1945].) And a sense of chaos, of a lottery-world without meaning prevails even where there is no overt mention of Nazism's devastation of the Western order ("La lotería en Babilonia," [1941]). Only a publication sympathetic to this vision would have presented it in a period when admiration for the Axis ran high in Argentina and more than one Germanophile applauded, if not approved, what the Germans were doing to Europe and its Jews. Indeed, reading the *ficciones* in their original setting—wartime issues of *Sur* full of material on fascism, Mussolini, Hitler, and the raging battle—there is a heightened intensity about them lost in subsequent recompilations. To cite one instance: "Tlön, Uqbar, Orbis Tertius" appeared in May 1940, the month when Hitler overran Holland, Belgium and Luxembourg. Victoria Ocampo, indignant at the fascist advance and at Argentina's neutrality, wrote a strong piece, printed but a few pages away from the Borges story, in which she declared that a world ruled by love, as imperfect as it may be, was preferable to a world ruled by the Hitlerite ideal of hatred and dictatorship ("El camino de America," 10, No. 68, 26). Such a context makes all too timely Borges's tale of Tlön, a man-made order, rigorous

---

[8] The following stories appeared in *Sur* between 1939 and 1946:
—"Pierre Menard, autor del Quijote," 9, No. 56 (May 1939), 7–16.
—"Tlön, Uqbar, Orbis Tertius," 10, No. 68 (May 1940), 30–46.
—"Las ruinas circulares," 10, No. 75 (Dec. 1940), 100–106.
—"La lotería en Babilonia," 10, No. 76 (Jan. 1941), 70–76.
—"La muerte y la brújula," 12, No. 92 (May 1942), 27–39.
—"El milagro secreto," 12, No. 101 (Feb. 1943), 13–20.
—"Tema del traidor y del héroe," 14, No. 112 (Feb. 1944), 23–26.
—"Biografía de Tadeo Isidoro Cruz," 14, No. 122 (Dec. 1944), 7–10.
—"El Aleph," 14, No. 131 (Sept. 1945), 52–66.
—"Deutsches Requiem," 15, No. 136 (Feb. 1946), 7–14.
Almost all of these have some connection to the times and often to things Jewish.

yet ruthless, determined to reshape every phase of life, and even rewrite the past to fit its philosophy. And just so that no one misses the connection, Borges explains in the spurious 1947 "postdata" to the story: "Hace diez años [i.e., 1937, the Hitler days] bastaba cualquier simetría con apariencia de orden —el materialismo dialéctico, el antisemitismo, el nazismo— para embelesar a los hombres. ¿Cómo no someterse a Tlön, a la minuciosa y vasta evidencia de un planeta ordenado?" (*OC*, 442–43)

Sur was a journal for the intellectual elite: *El Hogar* was a totally different publication. Full of news about the latest fashions, events of the social season and recipes for the creative housewife, *El Hogar* has been described by Borges as "a popular society weekly" ("Autobiographical Essay," p. 240). Nevertheless, the magazine did attempt to inject a cultural note into its issues. Well-known writers were invited to contribute articles. Two regular, alternating sections, "Libros y autores de idioma español" and "Libros y autores extranjeros," brought news of local and international literature to the readers. In October, 1936, Borges became editor of the foreign books and authors page. For the next three years, from this somewhat unlikely spot, he sounded forth on matters literary, leaving behind what Rodríguez Monegal has called "the best possible introduction to his mind and work" (*Biography*, p. 288).

As in the case of *Sur*, an examination of "Libros y autores extranjeros" reveals that Nazism, anti-Semitism and militarism were very much on Borges's mind in this prewar period. The section is peppered with disapproving, caustic references to Hitler's debasement of German culture (often by eliminating the names and works of the Jewish writers Borges was fond of); to the vicious attacks on Jews; and to the cult of violence characteristic of fascism.[9] Concomitantly, there are

---

[9] See, for example, the comments of October 21, 1938, on the exclusion of Heine from a new history of German literature and the "compensatory" inclusion of the "acclaimed writers," Hitler and Goebbels (p. 89); the barbs of May 28, 1937, about the anti-Semitic children's book, *Trau keinem Jud bei seinen Eid*, (p. 26); and the September 3, 1937, review of Aldus Huxley's *An Encyclopedia of Pacifism* in which Borges quotes approvingly of the British

many items devoted to Jewish writers—Franz Werfel, Elmer Rice, Franz Kafka, Heinrich Heine, Edna Ferber—and multiple allusions to Spinoza, the Bible and Gustav Meyrink. [10] Thus, it was not only Borges's open—sarcastic—attacks on Nazi teachings which lay bare his viewpoint; the approving outlook towards a heritage vilified by a powerful teaching on the march also constituted a position-taking.

By July, 1939 Borges's tenure as editor of "Libros y autores extranjeros" was ended. Perhaps the magazine's directorship had come to the conclusion that his interests didn't really harmonize with those of their social-butterfly feminine readers. Despite this outcome, a few months later Borges was back in *El Hogar*, now on its front page (December 13, 1940). The article he wrote, entitled "Definición del germanófilo," and apparently his last for the magazine, was one of the most powerful assaults on Nazism to come from the author's pen. In it, Borges addresses himself to the local scene, to the Argentine partisans of the Reich who call themselves lovers of Germany yet are totally ignorant of the German culture Borges knew so well. Rather than Germanophiles, Borges argues, these people are anti-Semites, Anglophobes, Hitlerites delighting in evil. Among their aims, he observes, is the expulsion from Argentina of the largely German-Slavic Jewish community, which speaks Yiddish, a German dialect, and has mostly Germanic surnames: Rosenblatt, Grünberg, Nierenstein, Lilienthal. His respect for them borders on zero. The rise of Hitler may have some historical justification, Borges concludes in his article; Germanophiles have none.

---

author's call to resist evil not through "muscle" and "diabolic armaments," but through moral bravery (p. 30).
   [10] The dates of the references and allusions are:
—Franz Werfel—16 Apr. 1937, p. 28.
—Elmer Rice—1 Apr. 1938, p. 26
—Franz Kafka—6 Aug. 1937, p. 24; 29 Oct. 1937, p. 28; 27 May 1938, p. 24;
   8 July 1938, p. 28
—Heinrich Heine—5 Aug. 1938, p. 24
—Edna Ferber—2 Sept. 1938, p. 24
—Baruch Spinoza—20 Aug. 1927, p. 76; 8 July 1938, p. 28
—the Bible—24 Dec. 1937, p. 24; 2 Sept. 1938, p. 24
—Gustav Meyrink—16 Oct. 1936, p. 78; 29 Apr. 1938, p. 24

In the same year that "Definición del germanófilo" appeared, Borges gave yet another sample of his thinking on Nazism. Again, the instrument was the written word, this time in the form of a foreword to a book of poems. The author of the volume, entitled *Mester de judería*, was Carlos M. Grünberg, whom Borges knew from the *Martín Fierro* days.[11] (One of the Judeo-German names Borges cites in "Definición del germanófilo" is Grünberg.[12]) Grünberg's verses in this collection, Borges says in his introduction, give voice to the "honor and pain of being Jewish in the perverse, unbelievable world of 1940" (p. 78). They are the protest against anti-Semitism, and not only the European variety, but the homegrown, Argentine kind. *Mester de judería* (the title is a play on the medieval *mester de juglaría*: this is the art of Jews, not of minstrels) represents a new phase in Argentine-Jewish literature, which had earlier been characterized by a "grateful immigrant" tone. Here, Grünberg is not the insecure greenhorn anxious to be accepted by Argentine society and little disposed to criticize the land of hope. He is a full-fledged citizen unafraid to censure what he considers a perversion of the Argentine spirit. Borges echoes this aspect of the book in his introduction. Noting that Hitler has no lack of followers in Argentina, he remarks:

En las lúcidas páginas de este libro, Grünberg refuta con poderosa pasión los mitos y falacias que ese impostor y sus prosélitos han predicado al mundo. A pesar del patíbulo y de la horca . . . el antisemitismo no se libra de ser ridículo . . . En Alemania cuya lengua literaria se basa en la versión de textos hebreos que ha legado Lutero, Hitler no hace otra cosa que exacerbar un odio

---

[11] Carlos M. Grünberg, *Mester de judería*, pref. Jorge Luis Borges (Buenos Aires: Argirópolis, 1940). Borges's introduction was reprinted in *Prólogos, con un prólogo de prólogos* (Buenos Aires: Torres Agüero, 1975), pp. 77–80, from which I quote.

[12] Rosenblatt and Nierenstein were also names of Judeo-Argentine intellectuals. Angel Rosenblat (sic) was a distinguished philologist who in July, 1942, contributed a piece to the "Desagravio a Borges" organized by *Sur* (12, No. 94 [July 1942], 7–34) after Borges was denied the first prize in the annual literary competition sponsored by the Buenos Aires municipality. Mauricio Nierenstein was a contributor to *Síntesis*, a journal on whose editorial board Borges served.

preexistente; el antisemitismo argentino viene a ser un facsímil atolondrado que ignora lo étnico y lo histórico. (p. 77)

Borges has only words of praise for the poet Grünberg, to whom he refers—flying in the face of the Germanophiles—as "unmistakably Argentine" (p. 78). His admiration for *Mester de judería* is based on form *and* content (a distinction Borges rejects but still makes), on its "metrical dexterity" and "delicate passion, " on its "algebra" and its "fire" (pp. 79–80).[13] For close to a decade (1937–1946) Nazism forced Borges to focus on Judaism. Because the Third Reich made Jew-hatred a major item on its agenda and then embroiled the world in an all-out war, the question of anti-Semitism became inextricably woven into the fabric of the times. The "Jewish Problem" became part of a larger struggle between two antagonistic philosophies, and few could avoid choosing sides in line with their background and convictions. Borges was no exception. A descendent of Englishmen, a friend and disciple of Jews, then at the height of his powers and very much aware of events in Europe and Argentina, he felt it was his moral duty, particularly as a writer, a man of the spirit, to take a stand. He said so unequivocally:

Quiero añadir algunas palabras sobre un problema que el nazismo propone al escritor. Mentalmente, el nazismo no es otra cosa que la exacerbación de un prejuicio del que adolecen todos los hombres: la certidumbre de la superioridad de su patria, de su idioma, de su religión, de su sangre . . . No hay, sin embargo, que olvidar que una secta perversa ha contaminado esas antiguas e inocentes ternuras y que frecuentarlas, ahora, es consentir (o proponer) una complicidad. Carezco de toda vocación de heroísmo, de toda facul-

---

[13] The book moved Borges greatly. Speaking twenty-eight years later (1968) at a memorial act to honor the recently-deceased Grünberg, he recalled the afternoon on which Grünberg brought him the manuscript of *Mester de judería*; the emotion he felt on reading the book; and the impression two poems in particular—"Circuncisión" and "Apellidos"—made on him. He then proceeded to recite from memory portions of these strongly Jewish poems, which he had earlier included in his *Antología poética argentina*, coedited with Silvina Ocampo and Adolfo Bioy Casares (Buenos Aires: Sudamericana, 1941). During my conversation with César Tiempo, he described Borges's prologuing of *Mester de judería* as an act of courage given the anti-Semitic atmosphere of the time.

38

tad política, pero desde 1939 he procurado no escribir una línea que permita esa confusión. Mi vida de hombre es una imperdonable serie de mezquindades; yo quiero que mi vida de escritor sea un poco más digna. [14]

Though Borges struggled mightily to make some sense of the Hitler phenomenon—it is, for example, the exacerbation of a universally-prevalent ethnocentrism—the atrocities that Nazism bred forced him to conclude that it was uninhabitable. Because of this, there is no doubt that the Hitler years tilted Borges towards the Jewish people. Moreover, the tilt-to-the-Jews did not end with the signing of the armistice. So ingrained did the wartime dualities (England/Germany, freedom/fascism, Judaism/Nazism) become in Borges that he used them a structuring principle for his interpretation of post-war Argentina, the Argentina of Perón. Perón's fascist connections and the participation of anti-Semitic elements in the early stages of the movement he led were proof, in Borges's eyes, that the Argentine colonel was but a local incarnation of the Austrian corporal better known as Führer. And since there was a parallelism in perception, there was a similarity in response. During the 1930's revulsion at German Nazism served as a stimulus for the Jewish presence in Borges. A decade later, on a smaller scale, Argentine Peronism did much the same.

---

[14] These words were part of Borges's acceptance speech for the prize given him in 1945 by the Sociedad Argentina de Escritores for his book, *Ficciones* (1944). His words were published in *Sur*, 14, No. 129 (July 1945), 120–21. The main speaker at the award ceremony was Alberto Gerchunoff, whose speech appeared in *La Nación* as part of a long article on the gathering (14 July 1945, Sec. 1, p. 4).

6. Monsterfest

1945 was a momentous year in the annals of the West: the costliest, bloodiest war in history had ended with the defeat of the Axis and the triumph of the Allies. In Argentina, however, 1945 went down as the "decisive year" because it saw the rise to power of Colonel Juan Domingo Perón, a man who influenced the course of Argentine life certainly for the next decade and probably to this day.[1]

But if 1945 is remembered by Argentines more for Perón's ascent to power than for VE day, this does not mean the two events were unrelated. Both grew out of the era of fascism opened by Benito Mussolini in 1922. Each was a response to the militant philosophy which had swept Europe in the interregnum between the two world wars. The Allied victory represented one response to fascism: fight it and extirpate it from the body politic; the Peronist triumph exemplified quite another: learn from it and manipulate it as long as it is useful in your climb to the top. The fact that Borges was a standard-bearer of the first approach and Perón of the second, deter-

---

[1] Félix Luna, *El 45: crónica de un año decisivo* (Buenos Aires: Sudamericana, 1975).

mined the collision course on which the two were set from the moment the colonel became the master of what he styled the "New Argentina."

Perón's high regard for the fascist way at a time when Mussolini and Hitler were still ascendant was a product of his background and training. A soldier from the age of fifteen, Perón became a career officer, and in 1939 was sent to Italy to gain first-hand knowledge of Il Duce's corporate state. After two years in Europe closely observing the fascist process as it developed in Italy, Germany and Spain, Perón returned home praising Mussolini, admiring the national socialist "experiment," and itching to tailor it to Argentina's needs.[2] His enthusiasm was shared by a group of military officials who were—like Perón—nationalistic, pro-Axis and antidemocratic. In 1943, this group with Perón in active participation, seized control of the government through a coup, proceeding to rule Argentina with an authoritarian iron hand inspired by Mussolini and Hitler, and abetted by Axis agents and Nazi money.[3]

As such, policies of a fascist cut—muzzling the press, dismissing congress, jailing opponents—immediately went into effect. The Argentine Jewish community, already traumatized by the Hitlerite decimation of its European brethren and alarmed by the growth of anti-Semitism in Argentina since 1930, was subjected to an intensified campaign of harassment. Between 1943 and 1945, disturbances against Jews, frequently organized by young rowdies belonging to the Nazilike Alianza Libertadora Nacionalista, were common occurrences. The Ministry of Justice and Education was placed under the tutelage of Martínez Zuviría, the notorious anti-Semite and author of El Kahal, Oro, who clamped down on organized Jewish life, enacting a series of stringent discriminatory measures. So serious did the situation of Argentine Jewry

---

[2] See Félix Luna, Argentina: de Perón a Lanusse, 1943–73 (Barcelona: Planeta, 1972), p. 22; and Luna, El 45, pp. 58–60.

[3] On Nazi influence in Argentina at this time see George I. Blanksten, Perón's Argentina (New York: Russell and Russell, 1967), particularly pp. 40–42, 47–48, 277–281 and 400 ff.

seem, that the White House was moved to express "misgivings" at the adoption by Argentina of actions "so closely identified with the most repugnant features of the Nazi doctrine" (Blanksten, p. 226).

In this atmosphere, Colonel Perón consolidated his position as the real and only power behind the junta. In his quest for ascendancy over the Argentines he fashioned a constituency of workers, military men—and anyone else who would support his political ambitions.[4] Among these "others" were the ultranationalists with their Alianza Libertadora Nacionalista "storm troops," whose presence in the colonel's incipient movement gave a strong note of anti-Semitism to the opening phase of the Peronist era.

Largely thanks to the Alianza activities, gatherings of Perón's supporters in this period of consolidation of power frequently acquired an anti-Jewish hue and resulted in violence against Judeo-Argentine institutions. Assaults on university students—most opponents of Perón, and many Jewish —increased (Luna, El 45, pp. 211–12). On October 17, 1945, when the now legendary march on Buenos Aires by the Peronist masses took place (this march enthroned Perón as *de facto* ruler of the Argentines) the Alianza made sure to inject an anti-Semitic undertone into the proceedings, provoking protests from the Delegación de Asociaciones Israelitas Argentinas, Argentine Jewry's umbrella organization (Luna, El 45, p. 313).

Given these varied fascist affinities of Peronism, it is not surprising that its charismatic leader was seen as a Nazi by those Argentines fresh out of the anti-Hitler ranks of the just-ended war. Ignoring or belittling Peronism's face as a movement of vindication for the poor and underprivileged, the forces opposed to the colonel coalesced around the motto, "For Liberty against Nazifascism." The phrase expressed their

---

[4] Perón's courting of the workers even in this period of fascist supremacy (when he himself formed part of a pro-Axis junta) indicates that he already sensed the shifting winds of European history: that the age of Mussolini and Hitler would soon be over and that a new power base—not the traditional ultranationalist right—had to be formed.

view in a nutshell: the fight against Perón was the latest round in the world-wide struggle against fascism and its atrocious offshoots, racism and anti-Semitism.

Borges, in a declaration which appeared but two weeks after the events of October 17, made clear his total agreement with the opposition's stand:

> The [political] situation in Argentina is very serious, so serious that a great number of Argentines are becoming Nazis without being aware of it. Tempted by promises of social reform—in a society that undoubtedly needs a better organization than the one it now has—many people are letting themselves be seduced by an outsized wave of hatred that is sweeping the country. It is a terrible thing, similar to what happened at the beginning of fascism and Nazism [in Europe].[5]

In these words Borges shows his awareness of the fact that Peronism addressed itself to needed "social reform"—and this is one of the few places where he admits such redress was necessary. Yet he dismisses the movement's promises of social justice as just that, promises. In reality, Borges concludes, Peronism is no more than a Nazi-like "outsized wave of hatred." Hatred against whom? In addition to the traditional oligarchy, the Peronists directed their enmity towards democrats, leftists, university students and intellectuals—many of the same groups the Nazis had tried to suppress. But the Third Reich's greatest hatred, a hatred echoing in the formative years of Peronist Argentina, had been reserved for Jews. This fact had been seered into Borges's psyche during the Hitler years and now, as he equated Peronist and Nazi ("a great number of Argentines are becoming Nazis," i.e., Peronists), the anti-Semitic hooliganism of the Alianza took on an especially sinister quality in his mind.[6] His reaction took the form of a story, entitled "La fiesta del monstruo" (1947), whose central

---

[5] Borges's statement appeared in the Uruguayan newspaper, El Plata, on 31 Oct. 1945, during a visit to Montevideo. It is quoted in Biography, p. 391.

[6] Borges speaks of the Alianza terror in "Mil novecientos veintitántos," OC, 833. He also recalls the group as one of the horrors of the Perón era in "Un curioso método," Ficción (Buenos Aires), No. 6 (March–April, 1957), p. 55. This article was part of a polemic on Peronism that Borges had with Ernesto Sábato after the 1955 fall of Perón.

episode—a deadly confrontation between a Peronist gang and a lone Jew—is based on the Alianza attacks against Jewish students.[7] In this work, considered by Rodríguez Monegal to be the main text that Borges wrote against Perón, the contrast in the portrayals of the *peronistas* and the Jew (they are sadistic brutes; he is an independent-minded intellectual) leaves no doubt as to where Borges's sympathies lay.[8] Indeed, Borges made his point with such vehemence, that he was taken to task by a number of writers and critics who felt that "La fiesta del monstruo" exaggerated to a Nazi-like extreme whatever anti-Semitic "rumblings"—and no more than that—might have existed within Peronism.

Men like Juan José Sebreli and V. Sanromán, who criticized what in their eyes was the story's "absurd Hitlerian analogy," or partial view of the facts,[9] were members of a new intellectual generation that arose in the 1950's.[10] Though not necessarily out-and-out Peronists (many were Marxists), these young writers were attracted to the movement as a revolution against the past: an attempt to change the socio-

---

[7] "La fiesta del monstruo," *Marcha* (Montevideo), 30 Sept. 1955, pp. 20–23. The story, which Borges wrote in collaboration with Bioy Casares under the pseudonym H. Bustos Domecq, was later included in the Borges-Bioy anthology, *Nuevos cuentos de Bustos Domecq*. An English translation of the story appeared under the title "Monsterfest" in *Fiction*, 5, No. 1 (1976), 2–5 with an introduction by Emir Rodríguez Monegal. Alfred MacAdam, who translated the story with Suzanne Jill Levine and Rodríguez Monegal, has authored one of the few critical studies on the work, "El espejo y la mentira, dos cuentos de Borges y Bioy Casares," *Revista iberoamericana*, 37, No. 75 (1971), 357–374. The "monster" of the title is, of course, Perón, also referred to as "el múltiple monstruo" in "Un curioso método," p. 56.

[8] "Borges y la política," p. 287. Rodríguez Monegal reiterates the importance of the story in his *Biography*, p. 406.

[9] See Sebreli, *La cuestión judía en la Argentina*, p. 239; and V. Sanromán, "La fiesta del monstruo," *Contorno* (Buenos Aires), Nos. 7–8 (July 1956), p. 50, quoted in María Luisa Bastos, *Borges ante la crítica argentina, 1923–1960* (Buenos Aires: Hispamérica, 1974), p. 251. Another criticism of "Monsterfest" voiced from a viewpoint favorable to Perón is found in Ernesto Goldar, *El peronismo en la literatura argentina* (Buenos Aires: Freeland, 1971), pp. 34–35.

[10] On this generation see Emir Rodríguez Monegal, *El juicio de los parricidas: la nueva generación argentina y sus maestros* (Buenos Aires: Deucalión, 1956); Martin S. Stabb, "Argentine Letters and the Peronato: An Overview," *Journal of Inter-American Studies and World Affairs*, 13, Nos. 3–4 (July–Oct. 1971), 434–55; and Bastos, pp. 241–61.

political structures of Old Argentina with its privileged Establishment and dependence on foreign powers, into a New Argentina of greater equality among citizens and less vassalage to transnational interests. As such, they were less inclined to condemn Peronism's excesses, instead emphasizing that as Peronism evolved it purged itself of the Alianza Jew-baiting; and that under Perón Argentine Jews made strides towards greater political and social equality.[11]

Other factors probably also contributed to these writers' downplaying of the anti-Semitic notes in Peronism in contrast to Borges's stressing of those notes. One was age. Because they were younger than the author of "Deutsches Requiem," they had not experienced the Nazi era with such passionate intensity, and considered Peronist anti-Semitism more an immoderation in a time marked by a loosening of restraints than an offshoot of Hitler's Final Solution. Then, too, formed as they were in Argentina, not abroad, and entering the literary scene at a time of heightened national consciousness, they saw Peronism through the lens of their own milieu, or as they liked to call it, *contorno vital*.[12] From this localist perspective, the movement in general, and its anti-Jewish fringe in particular, were not connected to international fascism, a connection which was responsible for giving both the Hitlerite overtones so condemned by the anti-Peronists.

Borges, of course, was at opposite ends from this new generation of writers. Peronism was for him a movement of idiotized *Massemenschen* led by a demagogue.[13] He would therefore censure any aspect of it that he could, including anti-Semitism, which was in his eyes a prescription for grave

---

[11] See on this Sebreli, p. 238; and Weisbrot, *The Jews of Argentina*, chapter on "Perón and the Jews," especially pp. 229, 237, and 240.

[12] The name of the major journal of the new literary generation was *Contorno*, a reflection of its members' primary concern, which was to discover their identity as Argentines in the 1950's (Bastos, p. 235).

[13] For Borges's description of Peronism, see his statement of August 8, 1946 at the dinner organized in his honor by a group of writers after he was fired from his library job on account of his opposition to Perón. The text of his comments, "Palabras pronunciadas por Jorge Luis Borges en la comida que le ofrecieron los escritores," appeared in *Sur*, 15, No. 142 (Aug. 1946), 114–115.

trouble: persecution, murder, looting, rape.[14] Furthermore, with his cosmopolitan education and internationalist frame of reference, Borges related not only Argentine fascism, but also Argentine Judaism to a world-wide context: The confrontation between *peronista* and *jude* (Buenos Aires slang for "Jew") was therefore a replay of the recent confrontation between Nazi and *Jude*.[15]

Because "La fiesta del monstruo" denounces an anti-Semitism deemed so fascist-linked, it can be considered a continuation and a culmination of the antifascist polemic carried on by Borges in *El Hogar* and *Sur*. Yet despite the similarities between the articles and stories of the World War II years and "La fiesta del monstruo" it would be a simplification to classify the anti-Peronist tale as just another in a series stretching back to the thirties. Important differences give "Monsterfest" unmatched immediacy and forcefulness as a protest document, and explain why Borges concentrated his denunciation of Peronist anti-Semitism into a sole text as compared to the outpour of writings during the war period. While he had followed developments on the Continent closely for over a decade, chronicling the Axis-Allied struggle and decrying the Nazi solution to the Jewish "problem," Borges himself recognizes that none of the death and destruction touched him or his fellow Argentines in the flesh.[16] The pieces in *El Hogar* and *Sur* may have told of dramatic, painful events, but they were always second-hand experiences, things Borges heard or read about. Moreover, in no way did Borges suffer during World War II because he opposed Nazism or spoke out against anti-Semitism.

In contrast to this vicariousness, "La fiesta del monstruo" is a visceral, personal work. Although the story had

---

[14] See his comments in "Las alarmas del doctor Américo Castro," *OC*, 653. When I spoke to him, Borges reiterated his view that Perón was despicable in part because he was "a nationalist and anti-Jewish."

[15] ". . . el jude se puso de rodillas y miró al cielo y rezó como ausente en su media lengua," "La fiesta del monstruo," pp. 21–23.

[16] See his comments in "Entretiens avec Napoleón Murat," included in *Jorge Luis Borges* (L'Herne: Paris, 1964), p. 386.

Holocaust-related underpinnings, it reflected not distant European reality but immediate Argentine reality. Borges is mordant in his description of anti-Semitism in "Monsterfest" because it was occurring in his own country, under his very eyes. Then, too, "La fiesta del monstruo" is powerfully direct because the account of the sole Jew, like Borges a nearsighted intellectual who suffers because he opposes Perón, expressed in telegraphic, symbolic form the writer's true-to-life situation in the New Argentina. Borges, who until this time had only known through hearsay—books and friends—what it meant to be Jewish, suddenly fulfilled his own definition of a Jew: a man hounded for convictions not shared by the masses, yet clinging to what he thought was right. [17]

The very way "La fiesta del monstruo" was circulated and published indicates what it was like to be part of the opposition in the Argentina of Perón. Although written in 1947, "Monsterfest" did not appear in print till after Perón's overthrow in September, 1955. The eight-year lapse between creation and publication was a result of conditions in Argentina, where no overt criticism of the government was harbored. Between 1947 and 1955 "La fiesta del monstruo" passed from reader to reader clandestinely, in manuscript, while Borges tried to maintain dignity in the face of harrassment by a regime which knew how he felt towards it. That is why there could be no outpour of writings to decry Peronism and Peronist-linked anti-Semitism. At the time of Perón, unlike in the war era, Borges was made to pay dearly for his antagonism to a powerful philosophy on the march.

Forced out of his modest job at the Miguel Cané Public Library where he had worked since 1937, Borges was offered what was considered a more appropriate post: the inspectorship of poultry and rabbits in the Calle Córdoba municipal market. But the writer was not the "chicken" Perón had expected. Borges resigned from his position and, having no

---

[17] In the poem "Israel," Borges describes the Jew as "un hombre condenado a ser el escarnio,/la abominación," who "a pesar de los hombres/ es Spinoza y el Baal Shem y los cabalistas" (OC, 997).

other steady source of income, confronted a new career in a field which until then had terrified him: public speaking. Borges's entrance into the world of lecturing provided him with a new vehicle for reaffirming his interest in Judaism and at the same time for bringing the fruits of that interest before diverse audiences. In time, the oral presentation, be it a formal lecture or remarks made off-the-cuff, became a valuable instrument in bringing Borges closer to the organized Judeo-Argentine community. The many activities organized under the auspices of institutions like the Sociedad Hebraica Argentina at which Borges spoke on Jewishly-related topics attest to that. In this way, too, Perón "nudged" Borges towards *lo hebreo*.

Among the subjects Borges lectured on as he traveled throughout Argentina and Uruguay were Martin Buber, Heine, German Expressionism and the Kabbalah ("Autobiographical Essay," p. 245). In Buenos Aires itself, although the authorities usually insisted that a uniformed policeman be present where he lectured, Borges was able to speak and teach in two institutions, the Asociación Argentina de Cultura Inglesa and the Colegio Libre de Estudios Superiores. It was at the Colegio that he delivered the important lecture "El escritor argentino y la tradición" (1951), a presentation in which Borges once again postulated Jewishness as a code word for cosmopolitanism, intellectual distinction and originality in opposition to a (literary) nationalism of limited geographical and spiritual horizons. [18]

In "El escritor argentino y la tradición" Borges's purpose is clear: to define Argentina's literary tradition in order to guide contemporary Argentine writers in their task. The historical context of the lectures—Perón's Argentina—is not directly mentioned but is latent throughout. The choice of topic (Argentine, not foreign literature); the definitions of the literary tradition Borges discusses and rejects (those of the nationalists); his allusions to the lingering effects in Argentina of

---

[18] "El escritor argentino y la tradición" was first published in *Sur*, No. 232, (Jan.–Feb. 1955) and later collected in *OC*, 267–274, from which I quote.

48

the Nazi/Allied conflict; and his final Europeanizing, Judaizing pronouncement on the matter of Argentine writers and tradition all reflect the noncosmopolitan, nationalist and antiforeign tone of the New Argentina and Borges's attitude towards it.[19]

For Borges, the whole problem of the Argentine writer and tradition is in reality a pseudoproblem because there is only one possible—evident—solution:

> ¿Cuál es la tradición argentina? Creo que podemos contestar fácilmente y que no hay problema en esta pregunta. Creo que nuestra tradición es toda la cultura occidental, y creo también que tenemos derecho a esta tradición, mayor que el que pueden tener los habitantes de una u otra nación occidental . . . Creo que los argentinos . . . podemos manejar todos los temas europeos . . . (*OC*, 272–73)

In formulating this answer Borges takes issue with the xenophobic nationalists who want to circumscribe Argentina'a literary tradition to the gauchesque or to the Hispanic. He thus implicitly polemicizes against the right-wing conservatives who had made the warrior-gaucho a sort of protofascist idol, and also emphasized *hispanidad* as a link with Franco's Falangist Spain.[20] Borges likewise rejects the position of the "existentialists"—an oblique reference to the young writers of the Sebreli and San Román generation—who advocate what he describes as a kind of pathetic solitude, a turning away from Europe to go at it alone and create a new Argentine heritage without reference to the European past.[21] (Recall that the criticism of "La fiesta del monstruo" had to do with this lack of

---

[19] See Blanksten, ch. 10, where the author discusses what he calls Perón's "Nationalist Revolution" (p. 222).

[20] I study the evolution of the gaucho into a symbol of the right in my "Alberto Gerchunoff: ¿gaucho judío o antigaucho europeizante?" *Anuario de letras* (México), 15 (1977), 197–215. As for *hispanidad*, Blanksten notes that "Fascism combined curiously with such aspects of Argentine life as a sensitive interest in events in the Spanish mother country" (p. 38).

[21] Existentialism—via Sartre—was an important influence on this generation (See Rodríguez Monegal's *Biography*, p. 423; Bastos, pp. 280–82). Part of the existentialist posture was an emphasis on the person "who decides from the limited perspective of his particular life situation rather than from some universal vantage point provided by reason and history" (Maurice Friedman, "Existentialism," *Encyclopaedia Judaica* [Jerusalem: Keter, 1972], VI, 1041).

49

linkage to events in Europe and the concentration on the local scene.) His own position, Borges allows, is deeply influenced by what had happened in Europe during the thirties and forties. He says:

Todo lo que ha ocurrido en Europa, los dramáticos acontecimientos de los últimos años de Europa, han resonado profundamente aquí. El hecho de que una persona fuera partidaria de los franquistas o de los republicanos durante la guerra civil española, o fuera partidaria de los nazis o de los aliados, ha determinado en muchos casos peleas y distanciamientos muy graves. Esto no ocurriría si estuviéramos desvinculados de Europa. (*OC*, 272)

Argentina is an inextricable part of the Western world in Borges's view, and the Argentine intellectual therefore has a right to make use of all the West's great themes (topoi, symbols, archetypes). But Borges does not leave it at that. He recognizes that despite Argentina's belonging to the orbit of Occident, an Argentine is not the same as a Frenchman or an Englishman. His position vis-à-vis the Western tradition is of necessity more ambigious, less centered. In fact, says Borges, an Argentine is rather like a Jew in his relation to the heritage of the West—a significant statement in the light of the recent fascism, anti-Semitism and nationalism. Both live and create within the perimeters of that heritage and yet are not totally identified with it: they always retain something of the stranger in a landscape not entirely his own. This apparent handicap has been turned by Jews into an advantage. Jewish intellectuals have given so much to Western culture, have been such innovators in European civilization precisely because they are not bound by its venerable givens and time-honored postulates. They can thus question the accepted, overturn it, and in its place put something daring and different. Argentine and South American men of letters—who are already in a "Jewish" situation with respect to the West—should likewise put their unhousedness to good use, says the author, and create original, path-breaking works of art.

Borges's application of a "Jewish model" to the Latin American circumstance is his own; but the model itself was borrowed from another thinker he cites in the course of the lecture: the American Thorstein Veblen, author of a well-known essay on the preeminence of Jews in Western culture (*OC*, 272). Veblen (1857–1929), known mainly as an iconoclastic economic theoretician, had apparently impressed Borges.[22] He was the subject of a separate lecture at the Colegio Libre de Estudios Superiores; was quoted in "El escritor argentino y la tradición,"; and was alluded to repeatedly in Borges's speeches, interviews and stories.[23] To judge by these citations, Borges was most taken by Veblen's article, "The Intellectual Pre-eminence of Jews in Modern Europe" (1919), which was the American's reaction to the post-World War I campaign by Zionist Jews to establish a state in Palestine.[24] Though moved by the Zionists' aspirations, Veblen nonetheless saw their idea as an "experiment in isolation and inbreeding" (p. 468). Both Jews and Christians would lose out if a Jewish homeland were created: Jews because they would be robbed of the outsider status in European society, a status which has resulted in their "position of distinction among the nations" (p. 470); and Christians because they would lack the stimulus of this nonconformist minority which had repeatedly goaded their culture out of complacency into discovery.

Though he argued specifically against the "Zionists' enterprise in isolation and nationality" (p. 478), Veblen's attack was aimed, it appears, at all isolation and nationality. The Jew-in-dispersion was so attractive to him precisely because he was nonisolated and international. Borges, in adapting Veblen's thesis to the Argentine milieu was also using the Jewish example to condemn the nationalists' project for withdrawal upon themselves, in this case the Argentine nationalists' desire to limit writers to local themes (*OC*, 271). In contrast, Judaism represented universalism; it was connected to

[22] Veblen's major books were *The Theory of the Leisure Class* (1899) and *The Theory of Business Enterprise* (1904).

[23] See "Alfonso Reyes," *Sur*, No. 264 (May–June 1960), pp. 1-2; Mario Diament, "Una conversación con Jorge Luis Borges," *Plural* (Buenos Aires), No. 19 (Nov. 1978), pp. 5–7; and "El indigno," *OC*, 1029–33.

[24] The essay was first published in the *Political Science Quarterly* in March, 1919 and later collected in *Essays from Our Changing Order* (1934). It is included in *The Portable Veblen*, ed. and introd. Max Lerner (New York: The Viking Press, 1948), pp. 467–479, from which I quote.

an outlook that Borges in the course of the lecture calls "an irreverence than can have, and already has, fortunate consequences" (*OC*, 273); it was, in essence, Borges's philosophy as a man and as a writer. When he tells his interviewers that he is sorry that he is not a Jew, and that his books are "profoundly Judaic," he is referring in large measure to the Jew and the Jewishness of Veblen's essay.[25]

The era of Perón, then, served as one more spur for the Jewish presence in Borges. Peronism's fascist-related roots and anti-Jewish violence fed Borges's philo-Semitism, and its persecution of the writer increased his identification with Jewish suffering. Further, by forcing him to lecture, Peronism furnished Borges with new means for strengthening his personal contacts with Jews. This period saw a growing participation by the author in the cultural life of Argentine Jewry, as he spoke and wrote on the dean of Judeo-Argentine intellectuals, Alberto Gerchunoff; served as judge for literary prizes awarded by Jewish institutions; and became a contributor to *Davar*, the literary journal of the Sociedad Hebraica Argentina.[26]

In the post-Perón years such activities and publications continued to grow. Half a century of contacts, influences, and stimuli which had produced a significant Jewish presence in Borges recurrently found expression on new occasions and in differing contexts. Borges's Judaic experiences were largely behind him. His Jewish metaphors had all been formed, they were all there, unchanging, in his oral and written pronouncements. And yet, the book of Jewish experiences was not totally

---

[25] The two statements appear in "Siempre lamenté no ser judío" (an interview with Borges), *El Universal* (Caracas), 14 Jan. 1978, p. 25.

[26] Borges's words at the memorial ceremony honoring the recently-deceased Gerchunoff were published in *Davar*, Nos. 31–33 (Apr. 1951), pp. 104–06, under the title "El estilo de su fama," and later became the foreword to Gerchunoff's posthumously-published work *Retorno a Don Quijote*. In 1954, Borges was one of the jurors for the Premio Alberto Gerchunoff established by the Instituto Judío Argentino de Cultura e Información as an homage to the late writer. For his earliest contributions to *Davar*, see the poem "Delia Elena San Marcos," published in No. 50 (Jan.–Feb. 1954), p. 5.

closed. The final stage of Borges's career still held something novel: his visits to Israel. Borges, who had so admired Veblen's rootless, multicultural Jew, and had based his vision of Judaism on twenty centuries of diaspora, was now confronted with what Veblen feared would be the Zionists' "experiment in isolation and inbreeding." The writer's response to Israel added a new dimension to the Jewish element in his work, a dimension which at once reconfirmed and modified his understanding of *lo hebreo*.

7. *The Oldest of Nations Is Also the Youngest*

Early in 1969, invited by the Israeli government, I spent ten very exciting days in Tel Aviv and Jerusalem. I brought home the conviction of having been in the oldest and the youngest of nations, of having come from a very living, vigilant land to a half-asleep nook of the world. Since my Genevan days, I had always been interested in Jewish culture, thinking of it as an integral element of our so-called Western civilization, and during the Israeli-Arab war of a few years back I found myself taking immediate sides. While the outcome was still uncertain, I wrote a poem on the battle. A week later, I wrote another on the victory. Israel was, of course, still an armed camp at the time of my visit. There, along the shores of Galilee, I kept recalling these lines from Shakespeare:

> Over whose acres walk'd those blessed feet,
> Which fourteen hundred years ago, were nail'd
> For our advantage, on the bitter cross.
> ("Autobiographical Essay," p. 257)

For Borges, the contact with the living reality of Israel was the culmination of a life-long fascination with the heritage of Judaism. From childhood, when he was imbued with British culture's deep-seated biblicism (exemplified by the Shakespearian verses quoted above), to manhood, when the Nazi

54

assault on the Hebraically-based "so-called Western civilization" caused him to become a defender of Judaism, Borges's experience had been preparing him for the face-to-face confrontation with the old-new nation of Israel.

Borges went to Israel twice, in 1969, and again in 1971. On his first visit he traveled throughout the country, lectured at major universities and met with prominent leaders and intellectuals, among them Gershom Scholem, the great scholar of the Kabbalah whose work he admires.[1] From what he wrote in the "Autobiographical Essay" as well as from statements made during and shortly after the trip, it is clear that Borges was impressed by what he saw. This was largely the result of finding in Israel the age-old Judaic heritage (with which he was familiar) alongside the most up-to-date phase of the Jewish experience, nation-building (which was new to him). To put it another way, the Jewish state was fascinating to Borges because it embodied both a continuity with a timeless tradition and a contemporizing of that tradition.[2] This combination of the old and the new is of utmost importance to him (it is, as will be discussed later, one of the governing principles of his work[3]), and discovering it in Israel was cause for enthusiasm.

---

[1] Borges's initial trip to Israel took place at the invitation of its late Prime Minister, David Ben Gurion. The invitation was a gesture of recognition for the writer's growing international reputation as well as for his pro-Israel activities. In 1958, for example, Borges wrote the opening article for a special issue of *Sur* devoted to Israeli culture and literature under the title "Testimonio argentino: Israel," *Sur*, No. 254 (Sept.–Oct. 1958), pp. 1–2. In 1966, he became a member of the board of directors of the "Casa Argentina en Israel-Tierra Santa," a projected Argentine cultural center to be built in Jerusalem. See on this Juan Rodolfo Rosemberg, "Un reportaje a Jorge Luis Borges," *Eretz Israel*, 26, No. 290 (March–Apr. 1969), n. pag.; and "Leading Argentine Writer Invited," *The Jerusalem Post*, 15 Nov. 1966, p. 6.

[2] His statements on the subject can be found in Rosenberg and in the interview with Y. Tirah which appeared in the daily, *Ha-aretz*. During my interview with him Borges reiterated the same idea, saying that in Israel he had the "very strange impression . . . of being in an ancient country and in a new country at the same time . . . And both are contemporary."

[3] See the section entitled "Pseudepigraphy, Commentary and Innovation through Tradition" in Part II of this study.

But if Borges was impressed by the Jewish state as the land where Jewish history is both confirmed and changed, in the poem "Israel, 1969," inspired by his visit and published just a few months after his return home, it is the change, Israel as discontinuity with Judaic tradition, which concerns him:

Temí que en Israel acecharía
con dulzura insidiosa
la nostalgia que las diásporas seculares
acumularon como un triste tesoro
en las ciudades del infiel, en las juderías,
en los ocasos de la estepa, en los sueños,
la nostalgia de aquéllos que te anhelaron,
Jerusalén, junto a las aguas de Babilonia.
¿Qué otra cosa eras, Israel, sino esa nostalgia,
sino esa voluntad de salvar,
entre las inconstantes formas del tiempo,
tu viejo libro mágico, tus liturgias,
tu soledad con Dios?
No así. La más antigua de las naciones
es también la más joven.
No has tentado a los hombres con jardines,
con el oro y su tedio
sino con el rigor, tierra última.
Israel les ha dicho sin palabras:
olvidarás quién eres.
Olvidarás al otro que dejaste.
Olvidarás quien fuiste en las tierras
que te dieron sus tardes y sus mañanas
y a las que no darás tu nostalgia.
Olvidarás la lengua de tus padres y aprenderás la lengua
del Paraíso.
Serás un israelí, serás un soldado.
Edificarás la patria con ciénagas; la levantarás con
desiertos.
Trabajará contigo tu hermano, cuya cara no has visto
nunca.
Una sola cosa te prometemos:
tu puesto en la batalla.
(*OC*, 1006)

Israel *was* the oldest of nations; its language *was* the language of Paradise, of the West's venerable Text. But Israel was also a negation of one persistent feature of the Jewish condition:

Diaspora and all that it meant.[4] Borges probably emphasized this untraditional side of the Jewish state in "Israel, 1969" because it was the innovation, an aspect of *lo hebreo* little known to him. The opening section of the poem, which evokes the Jew huddled in the *judería*, alone with his liturgies and with his God, contains the more familiar image, the one consecrated by the centuries. It was an image Borges had manipulated artistically as early as 1923, when, in one of his first works on a Jewish theme, the poem "Judería," he describes the frightened and defenseless Jews of some European ghetto awaiting the onset of a pogrom:

Ante el portón la chusma se ha vestido de injurias
        como quien se envuelve en un trapo.
Dios se ha perdido y desesperaciones de miradas lo
        buscan.
Presintiendo horror de matanzas los mundos han suspendido
        el aliento.
Alguna voz proclama su fe: *Dios el Eterno, Dios de
        dioses, es Uno*.
Y arrecia la muchedumbre cristiana con un pogrom en los
        puños.[5]

Decades later, but a year before his first visit to Israel, Borges again described the Jewish theme as one of nostalgia and exile generally devoid of insolence and courage ("Homenaje a Carlos Grünberg," p. 28). What the direct contact with Israel did, then, was to propose a modified definition of *lo hebreo* to Borges, a definition that to judge by "Israel, 1969," he found congenial.

Yet only a year after his trip, in 1970, Borges published a story entitled "El indigno," whose protagonist, speaking for his creator, condemns Zionism for making the Jew a man tied to a single tradition and a single country, without the com-

---

[4] In the poem, tapping his familiarity with Scripture, Borges borrows an image from Psalm 137:1, used for generations by Jews to express their sense of exile and feelings of longing for Jerusalem: "By the rivers of Babylon,/ There we sat down, yea we wept,/ When we remembered Zion."

[5] "Judería" first appeared in *Fervor de Buenos Aires* (1923). It was later included in *Poemas: 1922–1943*, pp. 53–54, from which I quote. In the 1943 edition the poem is called "Judengasse."

plexities that have always enriched him (*OC*, 1029).[6] The contradiction in response can be explained in this way: on the one hand, Borges was genuinely fired by the sight of a new nation being created by the People of the Book, on the Land of the Bible, in the reborn language of Scripture. On the other hand, his regard for Jews was based to a great extent on their diasporic experience, out of which had come those things he liked most about them: internationalism, linguistic pluralism and intellectual preeminence. The thought that Israel might eradicate these almost archetypal Jewish characteristics and make the Jew a man like the others, nationalistic, monolingual and hence intellectually impoverished, did not sit well with Borges. That is why, despite his backing of the state and his satisfaction at seeing it, he did not, and still does not, consider himself a Zionist.

This mixture of excitement and misgiving about the Jewish homeland long antedates Borges's 1969 visit. In 1939, for example, at the height of Hitler's persecution of the Jews, Borges wrote a review of Louis Golding's book, *The Jewish Problem*, entitled "Una vindicación de Israel."[7] In it, he recognizes the Jewish contribution to German letters and repudiates Nazi anti-Semitism, but does not vindicate the plan to create a haven for Jews in Palestine—which Golding does, in glowing terms. In fact, he dismisses the idea rather disparagingly. Part of the reason may have been his previously-cited objections to the Jew-as-nationalist. But it seems that another factor, more political, and more of the 1930's and '40's, caused Borges's less than enthusiastic response to the Zionist project: his strong pro-British feelings. For Borges to side with the Zionists on the issue of Palestine against England, the

---

[6] Borges voiced ideas identical to those of Santiago Fischbein, the protagonist of "El indigno," in his interview with Mario Diament. He reiterated the same thoughts to me.

[7] Jorge Luis Borges, "Una vindicación de Israel," "Libros y autores extranjeros" *El Hogar*, 24 March 1939, p. 89. The book Borges was reviewing was Louis Golding, *The Jewish Problem* (Harmondsworth [England]: Penguin, 1938; rpt. 1939).

mandatory power there, would have meant to turn against his ancestral and spiritual homeland—a step he was apparently unwilling to take.[8] But once England had left Palestine, Borges began to show strong support for Israel, to which, he said, he owed a deep cultural debt, and which he also considered a bulwark against the Soviet-backed Arab states.[9] This support reached a climax in June, 1967 at the outbreak of the Arab-Israeli Six Day War.

At that time, Borges's concern for what he saw as the threatened existence of Israel found its strongest expression in a poem, "A Israel."[10] Through its verses he once more underlined the connection between the people of Israel and the sacred Book that is the fountainhead of Western civilization ("Sé que estás en el sagrado/ Libro que abarca el tiempo y que la historia/ Del rojo Adán rescata y la memoria/ Y la agonía del Crucificado"); and likewise speculated on his own possible Jewish ancestry, for which, as he had written long ago in "Yo, judío," there was scant documentary evidence, but which he now cultivated as a way of identifying with Jews ("¿Quién me dirá si estás en el perdido/ Laberinto . . . / De mi sangre, Israel?"). When Israel turned out to be the victor in the war, Borges again expressed his feelings in poetry. This second poem, entitled simply "Israel," had as its main theme the

---

[8] Information from personal interview. As late as 1965 Borges refused to prologue another book by his friend Carlos Grünberg, *Junto a un río de Babel* (Buenos Aires: Acervo Cultural, 1965), because, he told me, it contained anti-British poems written by the pro-Zionist poet during the 1940's.

[9] See Borges's comments on his debt to the Jewish people and Israel in his conversation with Sverdlik, p. 3. His ideas on the world-wide political implications of the Arab-Israeli conflict can be found in Fernando Sorrentino, *Siete conversaciones con Jorge Luis Borges* (Buenos Aires: Pardo, 1973), p. 116.

[10] "A Israel" appeared as the opening selection in *Davar*, No. 112 (Jan.–March 1967), p. 3. It is included in *OC*, 996. At the time of the Six Day War Borges also signed a declaration of solidarity with Israel and went to the Sociedad Hebraica Argentina, as he put it, to be with his Jewish friends at a difficult moment. See, Guibert, p. 352; and Marcos Ricardo Barnatán, *Borges* (Madrid: Epesa, 1972), p. 21. Rodríguez Monegal discusses the differences between Borges's position and the pro-Arab stand of Latin America's left-wing intellectuals in *Biography*, pp. 451–52.

tenacity of the Jew to live on despite persecution.[11] The final lines set forth Borges's conviction that the war was the latest phase of a ceaseless struggle for survival, a survival that had profound implications for him. They read:

Un hombre condenado a ser el escarnio,
la abominación, el judío,
un hombre lapidado, incendiado
y ahogado en cámaras letales,
un hombre que se obstina en ser inmortal
y que ahora ha vuelto a su batalla,
a la violenta luz de la victoria,
hermoso como un león al mediodía.

The State of Israel, recognizing Borges's interest in its heritage and its welfare, decided to pay him homage in a way intimately related to its intellectual life as well as to a quintessential facet of Judaic culture which he had long admired: respect for the book. In 1971, Borges was awarded the Jerusalem Prize, given biennially at the Jerusalem International Book Fair to those intellectuals from the world community who have "contributed to the Freedom the Individual in Society."[12] The author was cited by the award committee for his "entire *oeuvre* [which] is an expression of the freedom of the artist in society, an invitation to recreate the world."[13] Noting that Borges's writings were a "source of inspiration" to authors in Latin America and elsewhere, the committee took special cognizance of his "refusal to compromise with the limitations of language and petrified language forms." It likewise highlighted the fact that his creation "probes the labyrinths of the spirit of Man as Man" unbound "by geographical or historical borders of a particular state or people." At the same time, however, the committee recalled Borges's "special fondness" for the "spirit of Israel and of Jerusalem, and for the symbols which flow out of them."

---

[11] The poem was published as the opening piece in *Davar*, No. 114 (July–Sept. 1967), p. 3. It was later collected in *OC*, 997. Borges described his emotions of the period as the "exaltation" of the Six Day War (*OC*, 1021).

[12] Moshe Kohn, "Argentine Poet Borges Awarded Jerusalem Prize," *The Jerusalem Post*, 19 Jan. 1971, p. 5.

[13] "Jerusalem Prize Citation," *The Jerusalem Post*, 19 Apr. 1971, p. 7.

The State of Israel, then, rounded out and enlarged Borges's fascination with *lo hebreo* in several ways. First, precisely because Borges had been attracted to Judaism for so long, Israel served as a coming alive of the Judaic tradition, the places, people and things about which he had read or heard. Second, by confronting the author with the antithesis of the cerebral wanderer he admired, Israel modified his vision of the Jew. Though Borges's feelings towards the nationally-conscious, assertive Israeli were mixed, he was nonetheless impressed enough to take note of the new figure, and to incorporate him into his work. Finally, Israel, as the Jewish state living under the threat of destruction, was for Borges one more moment in the cyclical battle between Jew and anti-Jew, which had previously inclined him in the direction of *lo hebreo*, and, during the days of the Six Day War, did so again.

PART II

Introduction

> Dos tendencias he descubierto, al corregir las pruebas, en los
> misceláneos trabajos de este volumen.
>   Una, a estimar las ideas religiosas o filosóficas por su valor
> estético y aun por lo que encierran de singular y de maravilloso.
> Esto es, quizá, indicio de un escepticismo esencial. Otra, a presu-
> poner (y a verificar) que el número de fábulas o de metáforas de que
> es capaz la imaginación de los hombres es limitado, pero que esas
> contadas invenciones pueden ser todo para todos, como el Após-
> tol.
>
> ("Epílogo," *Otras inquisiciones, OC,* 775)

In the above declaration, afterthoughts to his major book
of essays, Borges alludes to the two main poles around which
his literary universe is organized. One is the esthetic use of
religious or philosophical ideas; the other, the reelaboration of
a few timeless fables and metaphors into an "original" writing.
Both these axes are—almost of necessity—closely aligned to
Judaism. Borges's introduction to sacred texts, the first source
of religious ideas which he could manipulate esthetically and
mold into an esthetics, was the Bible, considered by him to be

in its entirety a product of the Judaic spirit.[1] From Scripture, or from Jewishly-connected ideas about Scripture, are derived some of Borges's basic notions about literature, what it should deal with, how it should deal with it, and who its producers should be. From Jewish commentaries on Scripture—foremost among them the Kabbalah—are drawn other cardinal points of Borges's view of the literary craft, its importance, its subject matter, its methodology.[2]

In addition to providing raw material for Borges's esthetics, Scripture and Kabbalah gave the author some of the long-lived metaphors and fables on which his writings, always pushing toward the Archetype, are based. "También se le ocurrió que los hombres, a lo largo del tiempo, han repetido siempre dos historias: la de un bajel perdido que busca por los mares mediterráneos una isla querida, y la de un dios que se hace crucificar en el Gólgota."[3] The *Odyssey* and the Bible, the Greek and the Judaic: these are the two purveyors of the West's fundamental stories, fables, metaphors and legends, the different names Borges gives to the same thing.[4] But while the Greek fountainhead is exclusively the Hellenic heritage of classical antiquity, the Jewish only *begins* with the ancient text. As already suggested, Borges fishes in the sea of the Kabbalah, a postbiblical source. This is augmented by the use of other Jewish fables and archetypal figures whose origins cut across the ages and the miles.

---

[1] During our conversation Borges noted: "The Bible was one of the first things I read or heard about. And the Bible is a Jewish book." In "A Israel," he also puts forth the view that all of Scripture—Hebrew and Christian, the story of Adam and the story of Jesus—is Jewish (*OC*, 996).

[2] I make these statements about Scripture and Kabbalah as sources for some of Borges's basic esthetic ideas knowing full well that in a writer as encyclopedic as he is it is often impossible to trace things to one single, definite source. Nonetheless, the importance *he* attaches to the Bible and to Jewish mysticism indicates a) that they were powerful influences on his theory and practice of literature, and b) that he wants to be perceived as a writer shaped by Scripture and Kabbalah.

[3] "El Evangelio según Marcos," *OC*, 1070. The thoughts, expressed by Baltasar Espinoza, the story's protagonist, are also those of his creator. On Jesus as a Jew, see in addition to "A Israel," "Paradiso, XXXI, 108," *OC*, 800.

[4] Consult on this, "Los cuatro ciclos," *OC*, 1128; "Formas de una leyenda," *OC*, 740–43; and "La esfera de Pascal," *OC*, 636–38.

The task of the second part of my study is to examine the Jewish presence in Borges largely through the perspective of the two tendencies, which he himself suggests. The first half of the book looked at Borges's Judaism in the context of socio-historical and personal circumstances. Here, I will consider how Judaism contributed to Borges's esthetics and to his metaphors.

1. The Bible Is the Point of Departure for Everything

—¿Cuál fue su primer contacto con la literatura? — . . . debo recordar a mi abuela que . . . sabía de memoria la Biblia, de modo que . . . puedo haber entrado en la literatura por el camino del Espíritu Santo . . . (Vázquez, p. 35)

Again and again, in interviews and conversations, Borges cites the importance of the Bible in his formation. Consistently denying his belief in the doctrinal aspects of this, or any other sacred book, and frequently demonstrating this disbelief through the irreverent, parodic treatment of theological concepts, Borges nonetheless emphasizes and reemphasizes the esthetic merits of Scripture.[1] At the same time, as in the dialogue with María Esther Vázquez, he points to the connection between the Bible and his (coming to) literature.

---

[1] In the course of his dialogues with Ernesto Sábato, Borges said the following of sacred, or theological writings:

Sábato: Pero, dígame, Borges, si no cree en Dios ¿por qué escribe tantas historias teológicas?

Borges: Es que creo en la teología como literatura fantástica. Es la perfección del género.

Though a reading of Borges's works will reveal quotations of scriptural verses,[2] and the more significant use of biblical archetypes—for instance, Cain and Abel—the Bible made a major contribution to Borges the writer in the form of certain literary concepts and modes of expression that he has secularized into the imaginative patterns that shape his books. Among these is the idea of the *Ru'aḥ ha-Kodesh*, the Holy Spirit, and the textual philosophy found in the Book of Job.

A. The Holy Spirit

In his exchange with María Esther Vázquez Borges says that he may have entered literature by way of the Holy Spirit. The term he uses in his statement, *Espíritu Santo*, is a translation of the biblical Hebrew *Ru'aḥ ha-Kodesh*.[3] In the Jewish tradition the phrase became associated with the idea of the divine inspiration of Scripture, that is, with the belief that the Bible was produced by the *Ru'aḥ ha-Kodesh* speaking through or dictating to worthy men. Christianity adopted this belief,[4] and the concept—also known as the theory of verbal inspiration—thus became the "regnant" approach to the Bible in

---

(Jorge Luis Borges and Ernesto Sábato, *Diálogos* [Buenos Aires: Emecé, 1976], p. 34.) This impious attitude is reflected particularly well and to an extreme degree in *Dos fantasías memorables* (Buenos Aires: Oportet & Haereses, 1946), a book written under the H. Bustos Domecq name of Borges and Bioy Casares. During my own conversation with him, Borges alluded to the Bible as containing "the most fine writing done by different men in different periods." But when I asked him what he thought of the Bible as a *religious* work, he avoided answering the question, and began talking about translations of the Koran.

[2] Some biblical verses and the places they appear include: Psalms 98:8, *Inquisiciones*, p. 69; Job 40:16–17, *El tamaño de mi esperanza*, p. 51; Exodus 3:14, *OC*, 750; John 1:14, *OC*, 977.

[3] The phrase *Ru'aḥ ha-Kodesh* appears in Psalms 51:13 and Isaiah 63:10. "Holy Ghost" is another translation of the term. On the subject, see Alan Unterman, "Ru'aḥ ha-Kodesh," *Encyc. Judaica*, 14, 364–66; and George Foot Moore, *Judaism* (1927; rpt. Cambridge: Harvard University Press, 1962), I, 237–38 ff.

[4] For the meaning of the Holy Spirit in Christianity and its relation to Jewish sources, consult Benjamin Breckinridge Warfield, *Revelation and Inspiration* (New York: Oxford University Press, 1927), particularly, p. 177 ff.

Western civilization, retaining "its hold upon devout believers in both Judaism and Christianity to this day."[5]

As Borges's words to Vázquez indicate, his grandmother was instrumental in familiarizing him with this traditional view of Scripture, which was part and parcel of her Protestant faith. But just as Borges considers that faith to be fundamentally Judaic, with its biblicism an approach to the Hebrew fountainhead, so he sees the concept of the Holy Spirit as a Jewish one—though he is well aware of its place in Christian theology.[6] In one of his prologues, when discussing the way a writer is inspired to produce a text, he recalls that it was the Hebrews who invoked the Holy Spirit;[7] in *An Introduction to English Literature*, he again connects the *Ru'aḥ ha-Kodesh* to its Judaic roots, noting that Samuel Taylor Coleridge's father, a minister, "delighted his rustic parishioners by inserting in his sermons long passages 'in the very language of the Holy Spirit,' that is to say, in Hebrew";[8] and in a discussion of the Kabbalah he explains that its mystical doctrines were predicated on the idea that the Torah, or Pentateuch, was a sacred book, in other words, a book that the Holy Spirit, "yielding" to literature, wrote.[9]

Borges, then, says that he may well have entered litera-

[5] Robert Gordis, "The Bible as a Cultural Monument," in *The Jews: Their History, Culture and Religion*, I, 784.

[6] See his digression on the Christian aspects of the Holy Spirit both as Author and as a part of the Trinity in "Una vindicación de la cábala," *OC*, 209–11. A secular writer who Borges often cites as one interested in the esthetic merits of the Holy Spirit idea is Valéry. (See, for example, "La flor de Coleridge," *OC*, 639.)

[7] Prologue to the *Obra poética: 1923–67*, 8th ed. (Buenos Aires: Emecé, 1969), p. 12

[8] Jorge Luis Borges, *An Introduction to English Literature*, in collaboration with María Esther Vázquez, trans. and ed. L. Clark Keating and Robert O. Evans (Lexington: The University Press of Kentucky, 1974), p. 36.

[9] "El misticismo judío y las leyendas de la cábala," *Nuevo mundo israelita* (Caracas), 7–14 Oct. 1977, p. 6; collected under the title "La cábala" in Jorge Luis Borges, *Siete noches* (Buenos Aires: Fondo de Cultura Económica, 1980), pp. 125–39. During his interview with Y. Tirah, entitled "J. L. Borges—On the 'Holy Spirit'," Borges said that he learned the notion of the *Ru'aḥ ha-Kodesh* from Judaism. Tirah comments that Borges alludes to it "using the Hebrew term" (p. 16).

ture by way of the *Ru'aḥ ha-Kodesh*. One thing this obviously does *not* mean is that he adheres to the concept as a religious tenet. Indeed, in the mouth of Borges, a latter-day heresiarch, the statement to Vázquez has a sacrilegious, humorous ring, exemplifying precisely the kind of jocoseness with which the author handles theology *qua* theology. But in another dialogue, when asked about the impact of the Bible on him, Borges begins to elucidate what his words *do* mean. He says:

> All countries have produced fine writing, but I wonder who invented the idea that all writing came from the Holy Ghost . . .After all, you don't find in other literatures that kind of thing. . . They believed in the Spirit. They believed that the writer was a kind of scribe, transcribing . . . [10]

What strikes Borges most in relation to Scripture is the traditional view of the writer not as creator, but as amanuensis, not as originator, but as transmitter of something which comes from outside him, from beyond. The theory of verbal inspiration—Borges uses and discusses the technical term in "Una vindicación de la cábala"—deemphasized the notion of a text springing spontaneously from the author (originality) and rooted primarily in his "I" (subjectivity). Rather, as Borges says in the essay, the theory made the biblical writers "secretarios impersonales de Dios que escriben al dictado" (*OC*, 209). The two key phrases in his explanation of the poetics applied to the Bible, "write by dictation" and "impersonal secretaries," in effect describe the residue of the Holy Spirit idea in his work. The regnant approach to Scripture provided Borges with an antecedent for a dictated, impersonal literature which, when carried to its ultimate consequences became antiromantic, dehumanized, at once classic and modern.

According to the theory of verbal inspiration, Borges notes, God dictates what He wants to say, word for word ("Una vindicación de la cábala," *OC*, 211). If the Author, not the author produces the Book, then human literary originality is thrown out the door. There is no such thing as a writer who

---

[10] Personal interview.

sits down and in a vacuum, *ex nihilo*, creates. His materials are given to him. He just aims at reproduction, at setting down that which already exists. In the case of the biblical man of letters it was the divinity who provided such stuff as the text was to be made of. In the case of the Argentine man of letters, it is Literature, the production of his precursors, colaborers in the vineyard of belles-lettres, that "dictates" to the man from Buenos Aires what his text should be. Both the scriptural writer and the South American writer receive the Word. For the two, the ultimate literature is, in essence, "the ultimate transcription,"[11] a point Borges makes clearly and with considerable wit in his "Pierre Menard, autor del Quijote," when he writes that Menard's ambition was to produce a work that would be identical—word for word and line for line—with Cervantes's masterpiece (*OC*, 446).

The biblical transcriber, working with the Utterance of Heaven, literally had to produce pages which would coincide word by word and line by line with the Word. Borges, working with the utterances of men, uses the concepts "writing equals transcription" and "writer equals copyist" more broadly as metaphors of intertextuality, expressing through them his belief in the oneness, as opposed to separateness or originality of literature, with author building upon author and work upon work.[12] In the nineteen-twenties, long before Julia Kristeva's postulation that "tout texte se construit comme mosaïque de citations," which marked a focusing of critical interest on literature as a network of echoing, interrelated texts,[13] Borges wrote:

---

[11] Jeanine Parisier Plottel, "Introduction," in *Intertextuality: New Perspectives in Criticism*, ed. Jeanine Parisier Plottel and Hanna Charney (New York: New York Literary Forum, 1978), p. xix.

[12] Borges occasionally also plays with the literal sense of the Holy Ghost idea, saying that—as in the case of the biblical writers—the Spirit dictates to him what he should write. (See, for example, the prologue to *Elogio de la sombra, OC*, 976.) But since he does not believe in the Holy Spirit, his notion of the Spirit as the producer of literature is more related to the idea of earlier books "dictating" to later ones.

[13] Julia Kristeva, *Séméotikè: Recherches pour une sémanalyse* (Paris: Editions du Seuil, 1969), p. 146. I have consulted this edition as well as the two-volume

Es dolorosa y obligatoria verdad la de saber que el individuo puede alcanzar escasas aventuras en el ejercicio del arte . . . Esa realización de que . . . nuestros movimientos más sueltos son corredizos por prefijados destinos . . . es evidente para el hombre que ha superado los torcidos arrables del arte . . . Gloriarse de esta sujeción y practicarla con piadosa observancia es lo propio del clasicismo. Autores hay en quienes la trivialidad de un epiteto o la notoria publicidad de una imagen son confesión reverencial o sardónica de un fatalismo clasiquista. Su prototipo está en Ben Jonson, de quien asentó Dryden, *que invadía autores como un rey* y que exaltó su credo hasta el punto de componer un libro de traza discursiva y autobiográfica, hecho de traducciones y donde declaró, por frases ajenas, lo sustancial de su pensar.

("La aventura y el orden," *El tamaño de mi esperanza*, pp. 72–74)

Here is the same theme reiterated: artistic originality is a deceit; all art is not spontaneous but predestined; the classical (correct) posture, which is akin to the traditional view of Scripture, is that writing should be a palimpsest, what Kristeva called a patchwork of quotations.

Because Borges ascribes to this view, his "stories are allusions to other stories, his characters are allusions to other characters and their lives are allusions to other lives."[14] Borges's "El Aleph," for example, is among other things a reworking of Dante's *Divine Comedy*; his "El inmortal" reelaborates the Chronicle of Cartaphilus, the Wandering Jew; the golem is taken from Rabbi Judah Loew and Gustav Meyrink; and the essays—"Formas de una leyenda" or "Historia de los ecos de un nombre" are good illustrations—turn on themes traced through a myriad of sources and authors. If the biblical man of letters was an amanuensis, Borges is a librarian, constructing his literature out of words culled from the vast Library of the ages.[15]

At the same time, even as he uses the idea of the Holy Spirit as an important and serious esthetic principle, Borges

Spanish translation, *Semiótica 1—Semiótica* 2 (Madrid: Editorial Fundamentos, 1978).

[14] Ronald Christ, *The Narrow Act: Borges' Art of Allusion* (New York: New York University Press, 1969), p. 35.

[15] See John Updike's article on Borges, "The Author as Librarian," *The New Yorker*, 30 Oct. 1965, pp. 223–46.

(typically) is not above looking at it humorously, poking fun at the very notion he has adopted as a literary ideal. The seminal "Pierre Menard, autor del Quijote" illustrates this well. By thematizing the concept "writing equals transcription" the story points to its centrality in the author's poetics; and by carrying it to its ultimate—ridiculous—extreme the fiction becomes a parody, a spoof of Borges's own, earnest project. "Homenaje a César Paladión," another story in which Borges gives narrative substance to the notion of literature as copying, leans even more towards the jocular—as befits an H. Bustos Domecq creation.[16] Its protagonist, the imaginary *homme des lettres* César Paladión, raises the methodology of literary unity (author "plagiarizing" from author) to heights which supercede even those of Menard. His entire *oeuvre*, not just one book, consists of others' works, to which the humble Paladión, realizing that originality is a conceit, has simply appended his name (pp. 16–17).

Scripture, as seen through the *Ru'aḥ ha-Kodesh* concept, banishes originality; so does Borges. Yet both, even as they consider writing the setting down of transcribed stories, leave ajar a back door through which the mark of the individual can come in. Borges's poem "Juan I, 14," has El Verbo, the Holy Spirit, say with reference to its Sacred Writ:

> He encomendado esta escritura a un hombre cualquiera; no será nunca lo que quiero decir, no dejará de ser su reflejo. (*OC*, 977–78)

God dictates, but the human instrument, if not the originator, still puts something of himself in the text. The amanuensis—a word Borges uses in the poem—by his mere handling of the transmitted tale refracts it through the prism of his particular insights and idiosyncracies (Gordis, p. 786). This, and only this is what could be called scriptural and Borgesian "originality": refracting, emphasizing, distorting and falsifying the given.[17]

---

[16] Jorge Luis Borges and Adolfo Bioy Casares, "Homenaje a César Paladión," *Crónicas de Bustos Domecq*, pp. 13–14.

[17] See Borges's words in the 1954 foreword to *Historia universal de la infamia*, *OC*, 291. Cf. Kristeva: "Tout texte est absorption et transformation d'un autre texte," *Intertextuality*, p. xiv.

Closely tied to this scripturally-related deemphasis of the writer's originality, is the lack of stress on his personality. As the impersonal secretary, so often unnamed, he pales beside the Word. That Borges sees such "nothingness of personality" (the title he gives to an essay in *Inquisiciones*[18]) as part of the Holy Spirit concept is clear from his approving reference to these words from Valéry's *Introduction à la Poétique*:

> La Historia de la Literatura no debería ser la historia de los autores y de los accidentes de su carrera o de la carrera de sus obras, sino la Historia del Espíritu como productor o consumidor de literatura. Esa historia podría llevarse a término sin mencionar un solo escritor. Podemos estudiar la forma poética del Libro de Job o del Cantar de los Cantares, sin la menor intervención de la biografía de sus autores, que son enteramente desconocidos. (*El Hogar*, 10 June 1938, p. 24)

One example of a writing that does away with what Borges calls "romantic self-idolatry and vociferous individualism" is Scripture ("La nadería," p. 93). On its ancient pages Borges could find a precedent for what he set out to achieve around 1926:

> Quiero abatir la excepcional preeminencia que hoy suele adjudicarse al yo . . . Quiero . . . levantar . . . una estética, hostil al psicologismo que nos dejó el siglo pasado, afecta a los clásicos y empero alentadora de las más díscolas tendencias de hoy. ("La nadería," p. 84)

As Borges outlines it, this esthetic of impersonality—which became one of the mainstays of his work—has three facets. First, it calls for a knocking down of psychologism, that is, of subjectivity as the source and content of artistic creation. Like those who saw the biblical writers as impersonal secretaries, Borges believes that the major task of the author is *not* to let his personality hang out, but to concentrate on putting together the work ("La nadería," p. 90). Second, Borges's impersonal poetics advocates that literature become "prone to" the classics. This is another way of attacking egocentrism because classical writers, Borges says, have a collective view of

---

[18] "La nadería de la personalidad," *Inquisiciones.* pp. 84–95.

literature, one which stresses sameness and unity as opposed to difference and individuality.[19] Scripture, through the notion of the Holy Spirit as the true Author of the text, held a similar vision of *e pluribus unum* for him:

> You find the most fine writing done by different writers in different periods as classed in a single volume, the Bible. That's a very strange idea. And the title itself is plural: *Biblia*, the books. That's never been done anywhere else. I wonder how it was done? Well, they believed in the Spirit . . . [20]

As Borges correctly explains it, the Bible (Gk., *Biblia*; Heb., *Ha-Sefarim*, "the Books"), which is characterized by multiplicity—many books, many writers, a plural name—was considered a unitary work because it ultimately had one Author: the *Ru'aḥ ha-Kodesh*. What this meant in literary terms was that the Holy Spirit idea not only submerged the biblical writer's personality by reducing him to an anonymous amanuensis; it also undercut his uniqueness by making him a mere fraction of a larger whole. If, as Borges suggests, literature had to take on this scriptural-classical quality, then it had to become a writing which aimed at oneness: oneness with the eternal topoi bequeathed by the past; oneness, too, in its cut, with synthesis and abbreviation the major stylistic traits.[21]

Third, Borges, in presenting his antipersonalist esthetics says that it must be encouraging of the most wayward artistic trends of the times. These were a move away from overdramatization of personal sentiment and a tendency towards what Ortega y Gasset called "dehumanization," that is, an antimimetic art.[22] In "La nadería de la personalidad," Borges presents a positive picture of this trend, but, significantly, relates it to time-honored literary postulates:

---

[19] "La postulación de la realidad," *OC*, 219. Borges makes it clear in this essay that he uses the terms "classical" and "romantic" to describe literary procedures, not historical schools. He also discusses the classical concept of literature in "La flor de Coleridge," *OC*, 641.

[20] Personal interview.

[21] See Christ's description of Borges's style in *The Narrow Act*, pp. 1–11.

[22] I have consulted the edition of "La deshumanización del arte" (1925) which appears as part of Ortega's *Obras completas*, 4th ed. (Madrid: Revista de Occidente, 1957), III, 351–86.

La egolatria romántica y el vocinglero individualismo van así des-
baratando las artes. Gracias a Dios que el prolijo examen de
minucias espirituales que estos imponen al artista, le hacen volver a
esa eterna derechura clásica que es la creación. En un libro como
Greguerías ambas tendencias entremezclan sus aguas e ignoramos
al leerlo si lo que imanta nuestro interés con fuerza tan única es una
realidad copiada o es pura forja intelectual. ("La nadería," p. 93)

The most modern art was, in effect, confirming and
expanding the nothingness of personality that Borges had met
early on in the theory of verbal inspiration. The proponents of
dehumanization, like the proponents of the *Ru'aḥ ha-Kodesh*
idea, preached the primacy of scripture over scribe. But they
went even further than their religious predecessors, extending
the idea to the point of making the text into a separate reality
which, because it did not aim to be a photographic reproduction of its creator's or anyone else's life, was constituted of
concepts, archetypes and artificialities rather than of verisimi-
lar personalities. In their hands nothingness of personality
became a fact of the writ as well as of the writer.

On the question of impersonality, as in the case of originality, Borges's work took the path of the Holy Spirit. In his
writings he concentrates on "weaving dreams"—constructing
the text—underplaying the intimate (*Biography*, p. 185). That is
not to say that this dimension is inexistent in Borges, only that
it is less patent, diffused, intellectualized. His treatment of
sex—the most personal of human functions—indicates his
position. Love, eroticism, which were the centers of the ego-
centric Romantic cosmos, are secondary in Borges, and even
when they do appear—as they do—he tends to hide them
behind such an elaborate intellectual framework that human
passion recedes. (His "La Secta del Fénix," none other than a
discourse on copulation, is a perfect indication of that.) As for
thematic and stylistic oneness, Borges constantly aims
towards them. An emblematic fiction in this regard is "El
inmortal" where Borges compresses the two essential myths
of the two primordial civilizations into one man: Homer-
Cartaphilus, poet of the *Iliad* and the *Odyssey*, and chronicler of
the Crucifixion. Into the story's dozen pages he telescopes
volumes, making one compact whole out of fragmented words

from different ages and texts ("El inmortal," *OC*, 544). And as far as dehumanization is concerned, the very names of Borges's narrative collections—*Artificios, Ficciones*—point to his vision of literature as another realm, a realm of rigorously-organized symbols ("La postulación de la realidad," *OC*, 217). In such writing even character, that element often most "real" in texts that aim to be a slice of life, becomes an abstraction. For example, David Jerusalem, the poet in "Deutsches Requiem" is presented as a symbolic composite of various individuals, and the golem, the homunculus of Prague in the poem of the same name, is a sham being, created by another "made" creature, man (*OC*, 579; "El golem" *OC*, 885–87).

"The oldest of nations is also the youngest," Borges once wrote about Israel. The same could be said of the concept of the *Ru'aḥ ha-Kodesh*, the Holy Spirit as the producer of literature, in relation to his work. The oldest esthetics, that of impersonal secretaries that take dictation, is also the newest. And this is not the only area where Borges found the modern in the ancient. His innovative, contemporary writings have another biblical forerunner: the anonymous author of the Book of Job.

B. The Book of Job

The Book of Job, which he has known from childhood, has always been one of Borges's favorites. He numbers it among the world's literary masterpieces; alludes to it repeatedly in essays and conversations; includes certain of its motifs in his works; and makes it one of the topics of his lectures.[23] Borges has a special predilection for this scriptural tale because the account of the God-fearing man from the

---

[23] Borges mentioned his fondness for the Book of Job to Vázquez (pp. 145–6) and restated it to me when we spoke. Allusions to the work can be found in the essays "Examen de metáforas," *Inquisiciones*, p. 74; "La adjetivación," *El tamaño de mi esperanza*, pp. 51–52; and "Sobre los clásicos," *OC*, 773. Borges also talks about the book in his dialogues with Sábato (pp. 34, 110) and Fernando Sorrentino, *Siete conversaciones con Jorge Luis Borges*, p. 115. Motifs from Job appear in "Deutsches Requiem," *OC*, 576; "Everything and Nothing," *OC*, 804; and *El libro de los seres imaginarios*, coauthored with Margarita Guerrero (Buenos Aires: Kier, 1976), pp. 39–40 and 137. An important

Land of Uz who suffers without sinning contains the theme and the technique around which he has built his literature. From the Book of Job can be extrapolated the basic conceptual and poetic propositions which give form to Borges's fictional cosmos.

In Borges's opinion, other interpretations of the ancient work—that it is a fable about the persistence of faith in the face of adversity, that it is an attempt to justify the existence of evil in the world—are wrong. Its true message, he insists, can be distilled from the closing chapters (38–42) which portray the Lord speaking to Job out of the whirlwind. Here, God challenges the pained Uzzite: "Do you know the laws of the heavens; / can you establish My order on the earth?" (38:33)[24] Humanity, the Lord tells the presumptuous Job, is ignorant of the divine principles that govern the world and therefore cannot expect a justification for suffering. This inscrutability of God and His creation, as Borges says, is symbolized by the mysteries of nature which the Lord proceeds to enumerate, climaxing with a description of two monstrous beasts, Behemoth and Leviathan (p. 102). (The pair are mythologized versions, respectively, of the hippopotamus and the crocodile.)

For Borges, the verses (40:15–41:26) picturing these two creatures are all-important, containing the essence of the argument. This is because "esos monstruos . . . , vendrían a ser, de algún modo, por lo mismo que son poderosos, monstruos, sobre todo incomprensibles (ya que no se ve qué razón puede haber para que existan en el Universo y que puedan servir a la economía divina), símbolos de Dios" (pp. 100–01). God and the universe are an enigma. Therefore, the way to represent them is by means of the enigmatic, that is, the monstrous, incomprehensible, uncanny or fantastic.

Borges lecture on the biblical text, "El Libro de Job," delivered at the Argentine-Israeli Cultural Institute in Buenos Aires, was published in *Conferencias* (Buenos Aires: Instituto de Intercambio Cultural Argentino-Israelí, 1967), pp. 93–102.

[24] Robert Gordis, *The Book of God and Man: A Study of Job* (Chicago: University of Chicago Press, 1965), p. 299. This volume contains a translation of the biblical text along with an extensive preliminary study.

The unfathomable (the problematic) portrayed through the unfathomable (the fantastic): such is the theme and the technique Borges discerns in the Book of Job. It is a postulate and a poetics which he makes primordial in his books. "Perhaps the most important of Borges' concerns," Ana María Barrenechea writes, "is the conviction that the world is a chaos impossible to reduce to any human law." And, to depict this theme, she continues, Borges utilizes a number of fantastic symbols: "the 'lottery' that dictates the destinies of the Babylonians, or the monstrous 'library' of Babel, or the 'palace' [labyrinth] where the lonely Asterion meditates."[25]

By connecting the puzzles of existence to a literature of puzzling symbols, the biblical Book of Job prefigured what Borges found so appealing in works of the fantastic genre. As Barrenechea (who considers the fantastic, or what she likes to call *la irrealidad*, the very essence of Borges's *oeuvre*) explains,

> publicadas ya las ficciones que lo harán famoso, Borges sintetizó en sus conferencias sobre literatura fantástica lo que le parecía esencial en las obras del género y encontró que su valor fundamental reside en ser símbolos de problemas humanos universales.[26]

Borges's essay on H. G. Wells, one of the science-fiction authors he admires most, confirms and illustrates this linkage of problems and uncanny symbols, which for him lies at the heart of the fantastic:

> En mi opinión, la precedencia de las primeras novelas de Wells— *The Island of Dr. Moreau*, verbigracia, o *The Invisible Man*—se debe a una razón más profunda. No sólo es ingenioso lo que refieren; es también simbólico de procesos que de algún modo son inherentes a todos los destinos humanos. El acosado hombre invisible que tiene que dormir como con los ojos abiertos porque sus párpados no excluyen la luz es nuestra soledad y nuestro terror; el conventículo de monstruos sentados que gangosean en su noche un credo servil es el Vaticano y es Lhasa. ("El primer Wells," *OC*, 698)

---

[25] Ana María Barrenechea, *Borges, the Labyrinth Maker*, trans. Robert Lima (New York: New York University Press, 1965), pp. 50–51.

[26] Ana María Barrenechea, "La expresión de la irrealidad en la obra de Jorge Luis Borges," in *La literatura fantástica en Argentina*, coauthored with Emma Susana Speratti Piñero (México: Imprenta Universitaria, 1957), p. 55

As is often the case, Borges's approving descriptions of what others do in their books are really elliptical allusions to what he does in his. Starting with the central, Job-like mystery of the inscrutable universe, the man who takes credit for raising Argentine prose to the level of the fantastic (*OC*, 1144) extends the Jobian-fantastic methodology to other enigmas and processes: the question of Time and Death is represented in the odyssey of the tired Immortal; the challenge of taking in and classifying the Infinite is shown through the memorious Ireneo Funes; and the process of reproducing the species is portrayed by means of the spurious Sect of the Phoenix. Perhaps in this light Borges's frequent coupling of religious works and the fantastic can take on added meaning. The products of the religious imagination are not only fantastic because they are as unbelievable as Wells's invisible man, but also—and more significantly—because they have the same *modus operandi*: problems encapsulated in ingenious symbols.

This fantastic esthetics, which is fundamental in Job, is, however, but one aspect of a larger mythopoetic approach that informs the book. During his lecture on the biblical text, Borges explained this approach by outlining two ways of reasoning, "day thinking" and "night thinking" (p. 101). The first is logical, abstract discourse, which Borges identifies with the Greeks; the other, imaginative thought, identified as Hebrew:

> La imaginación hebrea, por lo mismo que era muy vívida, estaba acostumbrada a pensar por medio de metáforas, y por eso la lectura del libro de Job es difícil. A veces uno no sigue facilmente los argumentos: Job y sus amigos no discuten directamente, emplean palabras abstractas, imágenes como aquellas que he citado sobre "la patria de la nieve," "los párpados de la mañana" o "el monstruo que puede beber de un trago el río Jordán." Es decir, en el Libro de Job tendríamos una tentativa, una antigua tentativa de pensar de un modo abstracto pero el autor es, ante todo . . . un gran poeta . . . En el Libro de Job, el poeta está razonando, pero, felizmente para nosotros, está poetizando. (p. 102)

Razonar poetizando: that is how the ancient author of Job presents his case. He is obviously making statements about God, people and the universe, yet does so without taking the way of philosophy. Rather, he walks the path of mythology—expressing ideas through poetic structures—which for Borges is the path of literature.[27] The scriptural writer's tools are all manner of literary construction: image, metaphor, as well as parable and fable.[28] By means of these he presents the fruits of his speculations, even as he creates a thing of beauty. And, because he speaks in symbols, his thoughts are conveyed not explicitly, but through suggestion. This too, Borges believes, is a lesson the writer can learn from the weaver of myths since mythology is one of those things which can produce the "imminence of a revelation" considered by Borges to be the esthetic fact ("La muralla y los libros," *OC*, 635).

Borges's art practices the esthetics of reasoning poetically which he identifies as fundamental in Job. No one more than he roots his writing in the philosophical and the theological; yet no one more than he consistently refuses to be labeled a philosopher, someone devoted to the systematic and abstract analysis of first principles and great truths.[29] What Borges does is to turn such ideas that appeal to him into imaginative creations. He presents his meditations on the perplexities of existence, which are fueled by and filtered through multiple readings, as forms of literature.[30] Thus, the question of what is reality (Does it exist outside the mind of the beholder or of God?) is set forth in a poem, "Amanecer" (*Poemas*, pp. 43–45). Here, the philosophical speculation is made into an inventive phantasy with Buenos Aires "disappearing" at night because the sleeping residents cannot perceive it, and then "reap-

---

[27] See his comments in *El hacedor*, *OC*, 799. Two studies on the relation of Borges's work to myth are Milton Clement Fragoso, "Jorge Luis Borges' Mythic Language: Its Symbols and Images," Diss. New York University 1975; and Carter Wheelock, *The Mythmaker* (Austin: University of Texas Press, 1969).

[28] In the course of our interview Borges said: "In the Book of Job instead of logical arguments we have metaphors and parables . . . There are no real arguments . . . The whole thing is done by fable, by metaphor, by God speaking from the whirlwind . . . "

[29] See his exchange with Jean de Milleret, *Entrevistas*, p. 116.

[30] Borges says in his foreword to Ronald Christ's book: "I am neither a thinker nor a moralist, but simply a man of letters who turns his own perplexities and that respected system of perplexities we call philosophy into the forms of literature" (p. ix).

pearing" at dawn. Or, the problem of time (How can humanity cope with the fact of its mortality?) is introduced in "The Secret Miracle," where Borges suggests by means of a fiction, a tissue of images, that time can perhaps be conquered through the life of the mind. Or, the question of justice (What is the right code of ethics by which to govern life?) is presented in "Emma Zunz," where the author again uses a story, not logical discourse, to imply that all systems of justice are relative, good as much as bad.

As for the suggestive indefiniteness that Borges finds in Job, it, too, is a staple of his work. In his talk on the book Borges had explained that following the exchanges among the protagonist and his friends was sometimes difficult because they did not deal with their subject directly, but instead used abstract words and images. The same could be said of Borges's fictional texts. He does not string ideas and arguments one after another logically, and in explicit phrases; he insinuates them, letting them emerge obliquely from various images and from the overall symbolic design of the work. In "La muerte y la brújula," for example, the proposition that reason is a deceit is not discussed directly. It is intimated in symbols: Lönnrot's ironic nickname, *el razonador*; the letter signed "Baruj Spinoza" with the argument *more geometrico* which leads not to a solution, but to error. In "La Secta del Fénix," the whole tale serves as an extended metaphor of the sexual act, which is suggested in multiple ways, yet never called by its simple name. What Ronald Christ calls "Borges' art of allusion" is not only a matter of references to other works; it is, as Christ rightly points out, a matter of "significances that are hinted at, but not revealed" (p. 1).

In the closing words of his presentation on the Book of Job, Borges says the following:

> Es un libro enigmático porque trata de ese enigma que es el universo, que somos nosotros y porque el poeta piensa, naturalmente por medio de símbolos, de metáforas. (p. 102)

What we have here is a capsule definition of Borges's books and a summary of his debt to the biblical book. Job expresses enigmas through enigmatic writing, problems through the fantastic, ideas and speculations through suggestive symbols. This theme and technique of the ancient Hebrew text is the theme and technique of the modern Argentine writer.

2. A Vindication of the Kabbalah

Ni es ésta la primera vez que se intenta ni será la última que falla, pero la distinguen dos hechos. Uno es mi inocencia casi total del idioma hebreo; otro es la circunstancia de que no quiero vindicar la doctrina, sino los procedimientos hermenéuticos o criptográficos que a ella conducen.

("Una vindicación de la cábala," *OC*, 209)

The passage above, which has become a *locus classicus* for those concerned with Borges's well-known philo-Kabbalism, gives clues to the reason for his interest in Jewish mysticism.[1] He

---

[1] The author's fascination with the Kabbalah is the only aspect of the Jewish presence in his writing to have received systematic scholarly attention. I have tried to avoid undue overlap with the work of other scholars, by and large presenting my own insights and conclusions. In the notes I draw attention to areas covered by my predecessors which I will not deal with, and I point out where my comments expand on themes touched on by others. On Borges and Jewish mysticism consult: Edna Aizenberg, "Emma Zunz: A Kabbalistic Heroine in Borges's Fiction," in *Studies in American Jewish Literature*, ed. Daniel Walden, 3 (Albany: State University of New York Press, 1983), 223–35; Jaime Alazraqui, "Borges and the Kabbalah," in *Prose for Borges*, ed. Charles Newman and Mary Kinzie (Evanston: Northwestern University Press, 1974), pp. 184–211; " 'El golem' de J. L. Borges," in *Homenaje a Casalduero*, ed. Rizel Pincus Sigele and Gonzalo Sobejano (Madrid: Gredos, 1972), pp. 9–19; and "Kabbalistic Traits in Borges' Narration," *Studies in Short Fiction*, 8, No. 1 (1971), 78–92; Marcos Ricardo Barnatán, "El laberinto de los cabalistas," in *Jorge Luis Borges* (Madrid: Júcar, 1972), pp. 111–21; and "Una vindicación de la cábala," in *Conocer Borges y su obra*, pp. 57–66; José Isaacson, "Borges y la cábala, o el escritor frente a la palabra," in *El poeta en la sociedad de masas* (Buenos

does not believe in the Kabbalah as a spiritual creed, the writer tells us, but he does find certain of its techniques and attitudes pertinent to his literature. Because it wed speculations to symbols, deified the Book and presented its religious quest as pseudepigraphy and revisionist textual commentary, Jewish mysticism had much to offer to Borges the writer. Small wonder, then, that he found it attractive and that his books resound with its motifs, ideas and *modi operandi*.

A. The Corpus Symbolicum

In his multiple studies, Gershom Scholem, the eminent interpreter of Jewish mysticism and one of Borges's major informants on the Kabbalah,[2] underscores the "peculiar affinity of Kabbalist thought to the world of myth."[3] This affinity,

---

Aires: Americalee, 1969), pp. 149–56; Rabi, "Fascination de la Kabbale," in *Jorge Luis Borges* (L'Herne: Paris, 1964), pp. 265–71; Leonardo Senkman, "La cábala y el poder de la palabra," *Nuevos Aires*, No. 9 (1972), pp. 39–48; Saúl Sosnowski, "Borges y la cábala: la búsqueda del Verbo," *Nuevos Aires*, No. 8 (1972), pp. 37–47; *Borges y la cábala: la búsqueda del Verbo* (Buenos Aires: Hispamérica, 1976); " 'The God's Script'—A Kabbalistic Quest," *Modern Fiction Studies*, 19, No. 3 (1973), 381–94; and "El verbo cabalístico de Borges," *Hispamérica*, 3, No. 9 (1975), 35–54. The earliest reference to kabbalistic readings in Borges's writings is found in "Historia de los ángeles," *El tamaño de mi esperanza*, p. 67, where the author cites Erich Bischoff's *Der Elemente der Kabbalah* (Berlin: H. Barsdoff, 1920). During our conversation, Borges told me that the German work was the first book he read on Jewish mysticism (during his years in Switzerland), adding it was a "very bad one."

    [2] Borges has paid poetic homage to Scholem as a scholar of the Kabbalah in "El golem": "Estas verdades las refiere Scholem / En un docto lugar de su volumen" (*OC*, 886). The volume Borges most often refers to among Scholem's writings is *Major Trends in Jewish Mysticism*, first published in 1941, and made popular in the 1961 Schocken paperback edition. When I wrote to Scholem asking him to comment on his meetings with Borges and on Borges's kabbalistic stories, he answered with a warm letter, recalling his "very pleasant encounters" with the author, and adding: "Borges is a writer of considerable power of imagination . . . [who] does not claim to represent a historical reality [i.e., he is not interested in the Kabbalah from a historical point of view, as Scholem is], but rather an insight into what the Kabbalists would have stood for in his own imagination" (Letter, 22 June 1980).

    [3] Gershom G. Scholem, *Major Trends in Jewish Mysticism* (New York: Schocken, 1961), p. 22. Scholem discusses this subject at length in *On the Kabbalah and Its Symbolism*, trans. Ralph Manheim (New York: Schocken,

Scholem explains, resulted from the rebellion by the medieval mystics against rationalist Jewish philosophy whose unemotional abstractions seemed to them unsatisfactory for penetrating the riddles of existence. Instead, the Kabbalists sought to approach these riddles by reembracing mythopoetics. They created a *corpus symbolicum*, a body of irrational images which, to their mind, hinted at the often enigmatic workings of God, people and cosmos more effectively than any of the conceptual formulations of the philosophers. To illustrate: God as the infinite, hidden Source, the primordial Point that sustains all points, all of creation, was suggested by the motif of the *En-sof* (Heb., "endless"). This same aspect of the Divinity was also intimated by the Aleph, the first symbol in the sacred Hebrew script. The other side of the coin, the sense of the Lord's finiteness and presence in the world, was likewise indicated through an image: the ten *Sefiroth* or attributes by which God manifests Himself in the here and now. Among the most significant of these was the tenth attribute, the one closest to humanity, which was called the *Shekhinah*, and represented the feminine principle in God as well as His powers of stern judgment. The potency and mystery of the powers of creation, a quality of God that people seek to imitate, was insinuated by a symbol, too: the golem or homunculus. Another image, the *Shem ha-meforash* (Heb., "hidden name of God"), also alluded to the creation force inherent in the Divinity. By manipulating this Secret Name man could attain "divine" knowledge to duplicate creation or to pierce its mysteries; he could also bring about (his) destruction.

From these examples it becomes clear that the Kabbalah signaled a return to the ancient Hebraic-scriptural tradition of suggesting problems through metaphors. Borges's admiration and "aping" of the Book of Job had been based in large measure on this quality of reasoning poetically; from the evidence of his testimonies and writings, his endorsement and emulation of the Kabbalah relates in part to the same characteristic:

1969), in the chapter entitled "Kabbalah and Myth," pp. 87–117. David Biale in his study, *Gershom Scholem: Kabbalah and Counter-History* (Cambridge: Harvard University Press, 1979) also devotes a chapter to myth as an essential component of the Kabbalah (pp. 128–147).

> Lo que me atrae es la impresión de que los cabalistas no escribieron
> para facilitar la verdad, para darla servida, sino para insinuarla y
> estimular su búsqueda. De ahí la abundancia de mitos y sím-
> bolos . . . Y eso no se da sólo en los cabalistas medievales, sino en
> la Biblia, en el *Libro de Job*.
>
> (Sosnowski, *Borges y la cábala*, p. 16)

In these words, Borges reiterates the fact that both Scripture
and Kabbalah take the mythological path of speculating by
means of symbols. He also notes that Jewish mysticism had an
abundance of such symbols—a reference to the *corpus symbolicum*—and suggests what their purpose was: to insinuate
the truth; that is, to point to the enigmas, to give an inkling of
the inner workings, to allude to the fears and the doubts.

Because Borges believes that literature is in large measure the metaphoric exploration of philosophical issues, he
has adopted the formula of enigmas-expressed-through-sym-
bols which the Kabbalists used in their writings, and like them
created a *corpus symbolicum* to give voice to the essential ideas
or perplexities of his works. This corpus includes mirrors that
question our reality by conjuring up another reality—or irreality; tigers that evoke the beauty, cruelty and hidden, but
eternal key to the universe; labyrinths that are the expression
par excellence of the perplexity engendered by the cosmic maze,
at once structure and chaos.[4] Since this last motif exemplifies
Borges's theme and technique so well, it has become an emblem for the author and his work.[5] The Hellenic maze is
undoubtedly basic in Borges but the Hebraic Aleph, golem,
Shem ha-meforash and *Shekhinah* are also important, though
they have not as a rule been included in enumerations of his
images. Borges has made the Aleph the center of a seminal

---

[4] Emir Rodríguez Monegal discusses Borges's system of symbols in
Borges por el mismo (Caracas: Monte Avila, 1980), pp. 95–120. See, likewise,
Barrenechea, *Borges, the Labyrinth Maker*, where these symbols are discussed at
length.

[5] This is exemplified by the fact that some of the major translations and
studies of Borges's writings have been issued under such titles as *Labyrinths:
Selected Stories and Other Writings*, ed. Donald A. Yates and James E. Irby (New
York: New Directions, 1964); *Labyrinthes*, trans. Roger Caillois (Paris: Galli-
mard, 1953); and (Barrenechea's study) *Borges, the Labyrinth Maker*. Borges
himself has never used the word to designate any of his books.

story which recounts a vision of the Center, that Point where chaotic multiplicity becomes unity, and then, to emphasize the importance of the motif and its message, given the name *El Aleph*—not *Labyrinths*—to the entire volume;[6] he has used the golem in poems and narratives—"El golem," "Las ruinas circulares"—pondering the mysteries of creation; he has built a major fiction, "La muerte y la brújula," around the Secret Name, whose possession leads not to knowledge, but to death; and he has utilized the *Shekhinah* and its myth of exile from God the Father due to sin as a symbolic underpinning for his well-known story, "Emma Zunz."[7] By using the mystical motifs, Borges not only shows his interest in these particular symbols and the ideas attached to them; he also indicates assent for the entire poetics of the *corpus symbolicum* because, as Laurent Jenny writes, "l'allusion suffit à introduire dans le texte centreur un sens, une représentation, une histoire, un ensemble idéologique, sans qu'on ait besoin de les parler."[8] In other words, each individual kabbalistic image, being part of a larger system, is a shorthand for the network, for the whole.

There is an additional aspect to Borges's interest in the kabbalistic symbol. This is the symbol's inherently insinuating nature which stimulates a search for meaning. The Kabbalists, the author had said, recognized that since symbols don't "tell it all" or "tell it like it is" (sic)—which the plain speaking of logical discourse should—they incite a quest to uncover the truths hinted at. To the mystics, the search set off by the allusive symbols was religious: their metaphors were intended to be for the initiate "gateways to a path of spiritual life," as

---

[6] Rabi, in his pioneering monograph on the Kabbalah in Borges, points out that while Borges's French editors chose the title *Labyrinthes* for the collection, Borges gave it the Hebrew name ("Fascination de la Kabbale," p. 265).

[7] For a discussion of the meaning of the Aleph in Borges see, Sosnowski, *Borges y la cábala*, pp. 77–81; Alazraqui, "Kabbalistic Traits," pp. 90–92. On the golem, see, Rabi, pp. 268–69 and Alazraqui's " 'El golem' de J. L. Borges." The Secret Name is discussed by Rabi, pp. 269–71; and Sosnowski, *Borges y la cábala*, pp. 86–88. I study the *Shekhinah* in "Emma Zunz: A Kabbalistic Heroine in Borges's Fiction."

[8] Laurent Jenny, "La Stratégie de la forme," *Poétique*, No. 27 (1976), p. 266.

one student of the Kabbalah puts it.[9] The esthetic dimension was secondary, incidental. To Borges, the hunt set off by the allusive symbols also has metaphysical content because they ultimately point to human processes or problems, but the imaginative dimension is essential: his symbols are for the reader gateways to a path of richer literary experience. When he was interviewed by María Esther Vázquez, Borges suggested how:

> Borges:— . . . quizá sea más eficaz el procedimiento de insinuar las cosas que el de aclararlas.
> Vázquez:—La insinuación permite pensar toda clase de posibilidades; alienta la imaginación.
> Borges:—Y, además, permite pensar al lector que él es quien ha llegado a la conclusión y no el autor. (p. 165)

Insinuating symbols, by making the reader part of the artistic process (since she has to decipher them and reach conclusions as to what they signify) provide her with a more active, and thus more fulfilling esthetic experience. Pierre Guiraud confirms this greater efficacy of suggestion as opposed to clarification from the point of view of semiotic theory when he writes that a puzzle with markings that are too clear, or a work of art that spells things out through the use of stereotyped rhetoric, requires less receptor (player, reader) participation to decodify the message and thus bores instead of exciting.[10] "Telling it all" both the Kabbalists and Borges believe, is *not* the way to arouse attention, prompt an interpretive search and provide access to a more gratifying religious or artistic encounter.

B. The Absolute Book

Another major motive for Borges's vindication of the Kabbalah is connected to its book centeredness, to what Borges had referred to as the idea that the Torah is a sacred book ("El misticismo judío y las leyendas de la cábala," p. 6).

---

[9] Arthur Green, "The Role of Jewish Mysticism in a Contemporary Theology of Judaism," *Conservative Judaism*, 30, No. 4 (1976), 19.

[10] Pierre Guiraud, *La semiología* (Mexico: Siglo XXI, 1978), pp. 21–22.

For the Kabbalists, Holy Writ was the very core of all meaning. It was the "cosmic law of the Universe, as God's wisdom conceived it." Its structure was "equivalent to the structure of the world." All "essences both of the higher and lower grades, of this world and of the world to come . . . [were] to be found there."[11] As such, no object was more important to the Jewish mystics than the Book, and no task was more worthy than the study and interpretation (production of writings based on) Scripture.

For Borges, too, no object is more important than the book and no task more worthy than the reading and (re)writing of "scriptures." The Jewish mystics made the Text the center of their existence; Borges has done much the same. His metaphor for the cosmos is the library, as he makes clear in "La biblioteca de Babel"; his texts "weave and unweave" others' texts and often, as in "El jardín de senderos que se bifurcan," revolve around a text; his characters are frequently writers— Herbert Quain, Pierre Menard, Jaromir Hladík—whose destinies are shaped by their literary creations; and his essays— "El arte narrativo y la magia," "La muralla y los libros," "Del culto de los libros"—deal with the enchantments, significance and history of the book. It is this last essay, written in 1951, which suggests how the Kabbalah's veneration of the Book had impact on Borges's reverence for books, how the religious mystics were, in a sense, pathbreakers for the secular men of letters.

In "Del culto de los libros" Borges notes that for the ancients the book was neither a holy article nor an end in itself, but rather a belittled handmaiden of the oral word. To illustrate this idea, he recounts the many warnings issued in antiquity against writing, for example, the well-known one presented in Plato's *Phaedrus*. But, continues Borges, such anti-

<hr />

[11] Scholem, *Major Trends*, p. 14; Biale, p. 90; Abraham Joshua Heschel, "The Mystical Element in Judaism," in *The Jews: Their History, Culture and Religion*, II, 944. Heschel, an eminent contemporary Jewish mystic, is here quoting the words of the *Zohar*, the central work of the Kabbalah (I 134b–135a). I have consulted the same translation Heschel quotes from, *The Zohar*, trans. Harry Sperling and Maurice Simon, 4 vols. (London: Soncino, 1931–34).

pathy gradually gave way to the more current cult of the book, already typified in the seventeenth century by Cervantes, who read the bits of paper found in the street, and closer to our times by Mallarmé, who said that the world exists in order to arrive at a book. This newer, positive view of writing is summed up by Borges with the statement: "Un libro, cualquier libro, es para nosotros un objeto sagrado" (OC, 713).

The author's use of the phrase "sacred object" to describe the modern attitude towards the book, points at the kabbalistic contribution to the about-face from ancient disdain to current respect. A big step towards the sacralization of the written word was taken, Borges explains, when

> A la noción de un Dios que habla con los hombres para ordenarles algo o prohibirles algo, se superpone la del Libro Absoluto, la de una Escritura Sagrada. (OC, 714)

This is a reformulation of the idea associated by Borges with the Jewish mystics, for whom Holy Writ was no substitute for holy speech, but a self-justifying, equally-valid—probably more valid—expression of God's word. [12] If, as the Kabbalists believed, the Divinity was the archetypal writer, who chose to express His will through a scripture, then that scripture could not be contingent; it had to be absolute. It could not be dependent on anything else (be a means to an oral end), but had to be independent (the end itself). In "Del culto de los libros" Borges suggests a relationship between Kabbalah and the notion of the Absolute Book, that is, the self-justifying and therefore

---

[12] Scholem discusses the importance of writing for the Kabbalah in his article "The Name of God and the Linguistic Theory of the Kabbalah," *Diogenes*, Nos. 79 and 80 (1972), pp. 59–80 and 164–194. He says that for the Kabbalah writing is not an "unmanageable image" of speech—as it is for the philologist—but the "real centre of the mysteries of speech" (p. 167). He adds that according to the Jewish mystics, in the original Torah the writing—God's hidden signature—preceded the act of speaking, so that speech evolves from writing, not vice versa (p. 181). These ideas about the precedence of writing and speech as a form of writing, are mentioned by Borges in his lecture on Jewish mysticism (p. 6). Harold Bloom points to their similarity with Derrida's concept of the trace, and notes that while Derrida berates Western systems of thought for not considering the "radical question of writing," the Kabbalah—which is an Occidental method—in fact does (*Kabbalah and Criticism* [New York: The Seabury Press,] 1975, pp. 52–53).

ennobled book, when he characterizes the idea as a "mystical concept" (*OC*, 714). He strengthens the kabbalistic connection by devoting a long paragraph to Jewish mysticism's worship of the letter, its belief that the instruments of *all* creation were not God's spoken words, but the letters of the Hebrew alphabet as manipulated by the Heavenly Maker:

> En el primer capítulo de . . . [la] Biblia se halla la sentencia famosa: "Y Dios dijo; sea la luz; y fue la luz"; los cabalistas razonaron que la virtud de esa orden del Señor procedió de las letras de las palabras. El tratado *Sefer Yetsirah* (Libro de la Formación), redactado en Siria o en Palestina hacia el siglo VI, revela que Jehovah de los Ejércitos, Dios de Israel y Dios Todopoderoso, creó el universo mediante los números cardinales que van del uno al diez y las veintidós letras del alfabeto. Que los números sean instrumentos o elementos de la Creación es dogma de Pitágoras y de Jámblico; que las letras lo sean es claro indicio del nuevo culto de la escritura. El segundo párrafo del segundo capítulo reza: "Veintidós letras fundamentales: Dios las dibujó, las grabó, las combinó, las pesó, las permutó y con ellas produjo todo lo que es y lo que será. (*OC*, 715)[13]

What emerges from the essay is that Borges considers the Kabbalists major contributors to the cult of the book which marks modern civilization. By raising the Book to an Absolute, by emphasizing writing as God's own creative instrument, they paved the way for a vindication of literature. It was their mystical ideas secularized which helped make literature into a respected profession.

When Borges speaks in the essay of the concept of the book as an end, not as a means to an end, he adds that this mystical idea, transferred into the realm of secular literature, produced writers like Flaubert, Mallarmé, Henry James and James Joyce (*OC*, 714). The four authors cited here are the same ones mentioned together in another essay, "Flaubert y su destino ejemplar," where Borges notes that the French novelist's exemplary destiny, repeated with variations by the other writers, was to be the Adam of a new species: the self-respecting and respected man of letters (*OC*, 263). This means

---

[13] Borges weaves this kabbalistic notion (which Scholem discusses extensively in "The Name of God") into "La biblioteca de Babel" (*OC*, 467).

that Flaubert the modern, unlike the ancients, looked on the author and the book with dignity. Whereas in the past the writer was considered no more than a light-headed mouthpiece for some outside Power, Flaubert saw him(self) more akin to the awe-inspiring priest, ascetic or martyr. His creations were therefore not subordinate to anything: they were independent artifacts, as solid, praiseworthy and consequential as other man-made marvels, or even the wonders of nature (*OC*, 263).

The qualities Borges attributes to the four writers he admires are the essence of his own view of literature. The Kabbalists made scripture (writing, language, letters) their core of cores and end of ends because it came from God and best represented His cosmic creativity. Borges, no longer able to believe in the Kabbalists' God, nonetheless recognizes that their sacralization of the letter played an essential role in granting his task an honored place—perhaps the most honored place—in the human creative order. In "El idioma analítico de John Wilkins" he says:

> La imposibilidad de penetrar el esquema divino del universo no puede, sin embargo, disuadirnos de planear esquemas humanos, aunque nos conste que éstos son provisorios. El idioma analítico de John Wilkins no es el menos admirable de esos esquemas. (*OC*, 708)

It was the Kabbalists, mentioned elsewhere in the essay on Wilkins, who proposed the Writ as a mirror of God's universal scheme, the sum of the heavenly words, definitions, etymologies and synonyms which make a cosmos out of the chaos (*OC*, 707, 708). Borges, lacking the mystics' faith, finds this divine dictionary impenetrable, but the residue of their belief in "scripture" remains with him: *el idioma*, such stuff as books are made of, is, quite possibly, the most admirable human way of giving some structure and meaning to the seemingly purposeless flux.

There is another aspect of the Absolute Book idea that dominates Borges's attention. This is the notion that in Scripture, the Text written by the Holy Spirit, nothing can be haphazard or without meaning. If Scripture is indeed the product of the Divine Writer who knows all and sees all, then no facet of it can be without perfect order or infinite significance. It must be, as Borges explains in a key passage from his vindicating essay,

> Un libro impenetrable a la contingencia, un mecanismo de infinitos propósitos, de variaciones infalibles, de revelaciones que acechan, de superposiciones de luz.[14] (*OC*, 212)

As in the case of the Absolute Book as a self-justifying work, Borges's fascination with the Absolute Book as a perfectly-ordered text has esthetic motives: he is interested in transferring the mystic concept from the Sacred Writ to profane writing. This intent is really the point of "Una vindicación de la cábala," where Borges, after discussing the lack of contingency in Scripture, goes on to analyze the problem of haphazardness in various types of writing: journalism, in which meaning is ordered, but the length and sound of the paragraphs is accidental; poetry, where the opposite is true, and euphonics governs sense; and the texts of "the intellectual writer," whose work, Borges says, "remotely approaches that of the Lord" (*OC*, 211). Such an author practices a sort of heterodox *imitatio dei*, attempting to apply a principle of godly writing—the absence of randomness in the weaving of a controlled, complex and meaning-filled text—to human literature.

One of the men Borges mentions as an example of this intellectual writer is Paul Valéry, to whom he devoted a eulogizing essay significantly entitled "Valéry como símbolo" (*OC*, 686–87). What the Argentine prizes in the Frenchman, the essay makes apparent, is precisely his closeness to this aspect of the ideal of the Absolute Book. Valéry's texts, though of human making, approach the heavenly model, because they reject the "idols of chaos" and advocate the order and lucidity which characterize Holy Writ (*OC*, 687). In addition, they approximate the celestial paradigm because, like it, they have unlimited possibilities and significances. Valéry, Borges

---

[14] See on this idea Scholem's article, "The Meaning of the Torah in Jewish Mysticism," *Diogenes*, Nos. 14 and 15 (1956), pp. 36–47 and 65–94.

notes, uses each experience or fact to generate an endless series of thoughts, producing books whose ideological density and suggestiveness can scarcely be contained on the page (*OC*, 687).

For Borges, thus, the Absolute Book is a prototype of a text whose calculated structure is a vessel for a plethora of revelations. It is, in other words, a prototype for his texts. This quality of Borges's writing can be discerned from a work like "Emma Zunz." Here is a tightly-woven murder mystery with a precise beginning, middle and end,[15] a mechanism of seemingly straightforward causes and effects which is, in fact, teeming with other meanings. Chief among them is the retelling of the kabbalistic myth of the *Shekhinah*. Emma, her wronged and exiled father, and the embezzler, Aarón Loewenthal, reenact the mystical story of God's Daughter—the feminine hypostasis of the divine—who is separated from her heavenly progenitor and falls into the unclean physical-sexual world as a result of sin. Since the Daughter is God the Father's power of stern judgment, she proceeds to punish the wrongdoer through destruction and violence, without, however, restoring the harmony which existed in the happy days before the sin.[16]

Such lurking revelations recall to mind that the Kabbalists' Absolute Book—Borges's model—is not only a text with "manifold and even infinite meanings," but also one with a "hierarchy of meanings," some exoteric, others esoteric (Scholem, "Torah," p. 65). This is because in a volume with unlimited senses, all of these could not possibly lie on the most evident, surface level. Many had to be buried, and consequently only available to those with special learning or penetration (the Kabbalists). The Jewish mystics had two ways to express this idea. They either spoke of the several "layers" of meaning of Holy Writ, or they referred to the many "lights"

---

[15] One of the reasons Borges likes the detective story is precisely its ordered construction and lack of randomness (Vázquez, pp. 122–23).

[16] Another mythic strand in "Emma Zunz" is the story of the sacrifice or suicide of a god. See 'El 'Biathanatos'," *OC*, 702; and "Los cuatro ciclos," *OC*, 1128.

that shine within each scriptural word. In the case of the layers, usually considered four, these progressed inwardly toward greater understanding from the literal (outer) sense of the text to its allegorical, legal (Talmudic), and finally mystical (recondite) meaning. As for the lights, they, too, had a system of gradation, with increasing illumination the more one dug into the hidden recesses of the text ("The Meaning of the Torah in Jewish Mysticism," pp. 70, 74–5).

In "Una vindicación de la cábala" Borges evokes both types of imagery when he calls the mystics' Sacred Writ a book of "superimposed lights"; and in his lecture on Jewish mysticism he makes reference to the kabbalistic doctrine that there are four meanings in Scripture, which was considered a ciphered, cryptographic writ (pp. 6–7). As if to emphasize that his central concern here, too, is esthetic, in the course of the lecture Borges again cites a highly-regarded author who had previously used these religious concepts in a secular context: the Italian Dante, who pointed out that his *Commedia* could be read in four different ways, only one of them literal. [17]

The description of Dante is, of course, the description of Borges, whose narrative model, Ana María Barrenechea says, proposes a reading on different levels, from concrete facts, to archetypal forms. [18] These strata, Barrenechea continues, are in tension with each other, and it is the interplay of their diverse meanings which gives Borges's fiction its complexity and richness. The first, or surface layer is the literal, concrete

---

[17] Borges's admiration for Dante is expressed in many places, including Jorge Luis Borges, *Nueve ensayos dantescos*, introd. Marcos Ricardo Barnatán and Joaquín Arce (Madrid: Espasa-Calpe, 1982). The application by Dante of a religious literary model to his writing was, strictly speaking, not kabbalistically-based since medieval Christian exegetes had also come to regard Scripture as having a hierarchy of four meanings. (Scholars have postulated an historical connection between the two systems.) But Borges, while aware of the non-kabbalistic aspects of the idea, nonetheless associates it, and Dante's secularization of it, with Jewish mysticism. See "El misticismo judío y las leyendas de la cábala," p. 7; and "Emanuel Swedenborg: *Mystical Works,*" *Prólogos*, p. 157.

[18] Ana María Barrenechea, "Borges y los símbolos," in *Textos hispanoamericanos* (Caracas: Monte Avila, 1978), pp. 147–48.

97

story with all the circumstancial details which simulate reality (p. 148). But already at this most overt level, Barrenechea writes, there are indications of other levels, intermittent signals that point to a need for decipherment, to an ever more abstract, distant and elusive goal (p. 149). To translate this into kabbalistic terms: even as Borges operates on the exoteric level, he hints at the additional, esoteric levels of his narratives which must be deciphered in order to gain full illumination of their meaning.

Thus, in "Emma Zunz" (to continue with the example used earlier), the concrete story, the murder mystery set in twentieth-century Buenos Aires, contains clues that hint at the hidden mythical layers. One of these is the names of the protagonists. Emma is a shortened, fragmentary form of her father's name, Emanuel, which not insignificantly is Hebrew for "God is with us." The daughter, in other words, is a part of the father, a father who carries the name of the (Jewish) divinity. Their adversary, the miserly Loewenthal, is named Aarón, as was the high priest who constructed the Golden Calf, symbol of money worship and of the kind of sinfulness that brings grief into the world. The concealed archetypal strata which such clues betoken are, like the Kabbalists' hidden layers of Scripture, available only to those with special insight or specialized knowledge—not mystics, but educated, practiced readers who can penetrate the hieroglyphic character of the text. In "Tlön, Uqbar, Orbis Tertius," where the creators of the fictitious planet prepare themselves for the task by studying the Kabbalah (*OC*, 440), Borges intimates his adoption of this mystical *modus operandi* when he speaks of a narrative in which the author would leave such literary footprints that would permit just a few readers "the deciphering of a horrible or banal reality" (*OC*, 431).

"The deciphering of a horrible or banal reality." Borges adopts the mystical methodology described above, but this phrase, appended to his description of the methodology, points to the difference between his use of it and the Kabbalists'. For them, the penetration of the divine cryptography contained in Scripture could never be atrocious or trival for it meant the possession of the very key to the cosmos. For

Borges, who doesn't believe we can grasp this probably non-existent key, and whose interest in the kabbalistic technique is, above all artistic, the reality hidden under the surface of the text can well be banal—if the narrative economy demands it.

C. Pseudepigraphy, Commentary and Innovation through Tradition

> [In the *Quijote*] Cervantes se complace en confundir lo objetivo y lo subjetivo, el mundo del lector y el mundo del libro . . . es sorprendente saber, en el principio del noveno capítulo, que la novela entera ha sido traducida del árabe y que Cervantes adquirió el manuscrito en el mercado de Toledo, y lo hizo traducir por un morisco . . . Pensamos en Carlyle, que fingió que el *Sartor Resartus* era versión parcial de una obra publicada en Alemania por el doctor Diógenes Teufelsdroeckh; pensamos en el rabino castellano Moisès de León, que compuso el *Zohar* o *Libro de Esplendor* y lo divulgó como obra de un rabino palestiniano del siglo III.
>
> ("Magias parciales del Quijote," *OC*, 667–68)

Another point of contact between Borges and the Kabbalah is suggested in the quote from his essay on Cervantes: it is what the author calls elsewhere "the technique of deliberate anachronism and erroneous attribution" ("Pierre Menard," *OC*, 450). Borges, an assiduous reader of Scholem, apparently bases his comments about Moisés de León and the *Zohar* on information culled from this scholar's *Major Trends in Jewish Mysticism*.[19] According to what Scholem writes in his study, de León was a "renegade" from the world of medieval Jewish rationalism. He embraced mysticism and composed the *Zohar*, a kind of mystical novel, in an effort to find a more effective

---

[19] That this information comes from Scholem's book seems evident from a comparision of what Borges says about the *Zohar*'s authorship in "Magias parciales del Quijote," written in 1949 (after the publication of *Major Trends*), and what he writes on the matter in "El otro Whitman," dating from 1929. In the earlier text, Borges speaks of an anonymous, remote compiler of the book (*OC*, 206). It was only in the late thirties that Scholem put forth the theory, now generally, but not universally accepted, that Moisés de León was the *Zohar*'s author and that he wrote it in pseudepigraphic form. Previously, many scholars considered de León a possible compiler or editor of the text which supposedly had strata from different periods (Biale, pp. 116–18).

spiritual way for himself and his generation. This way, the Kabbalist believed, was the mystical reillumination of the "true core" of Judaism contained in the everlasting Torah, whose teachings many rationalists had come to question or reject. De León clothed his creation in pseudepigraphic garb, making it seem the work of Simeon ben Yohai, a revered ancient interpreter and teacher of Scripture, precisely because he was interested in emphasizing the continuity and eternity of tradition, in underlining its never-ending authority. By attributing the *Zohar* to the Palestinian sage, de León was in effect saying that the mystical doctrines propounded in the book were neither novel nor radical, but "old as the hills" (*On the Kabbalah and Its Symbolism*, p. 95). They were no more than reformulations of accepted truths articulated long ago by venerated rabbis. They were Kabbalah, which in Hebrew means "tradition."

But many of de León's doctrines were, in fact, novel and radical. They represented an ideology—Kabbalism—which came "to the rescue of the tradition by giving it a new interpretation" (Biale, p. 120). The symbolism of the *En-sof* and the *Sefiroth*, for example, or the idea that every word in the Torah had esoteric meaning, were both central to the *Zohar*—and totally alien to the time of Simeon ben Yohai. They reflected not the ancient era of the Palestinian master but the medieval period of the Spanish mystic trying to effect an *aggiornamento*, an updating of a time-honored heritage by pouring new wine into old bottles. Pseudepigraphy was thus not only a way of stressing the continuity of an eternal legacy; it was also a "means for legitimizing creative work" as part of that legacy. Through pseudepigraphy the "authority of tradition is recognized, but the freedom of literary creativity is preserved" (Biale, p. 119).

In "Magias parciales del Quijote," Borges, having read and digested Scholem's views, makes use of the scholar's "whats" but not of his "whys." He reproduces Scholem's assertions concerning the *Zohar*'s pseudepigraphal authorship, but omits the reasons advanced to explain this authorship. Instead, Borges utilizes de León's mystification to suit *his*

100

ends, turning it into an early example of the confusion between fact and fiction, between reality and irreality which marks the work of writers like Carlyle and Cervantes.[20] The *Zohar* is seen by Borges as a predecessor of *Sartor Resartus* and the *Quijote*, books whose pseudepigraphy—a type of unreality that undercuts the author's identity—is a means for pointing to the illusoriness or instability of all reality.[21]

Viewed in this light, the Castilian Kabbalist is also a precursor of the Argentine storyteller, whose books are, to a great extent, the chronicle of the search for simulacra that confirm the hallucinatory nature of existence. One of Borges's favorite methods for inducing a feeling of unreality is the technique of deliberate anachronism and erroneous attribution—Moisés de León's technique. In many of his texts Borges the author disappears, and another, apocryphal "writer" takes over. "El inmortal" is presented as a manuscript written by the imaginary antiques dealer, Joseph Cartaphilus, who is an avatar of two ancient personages, Homer and the Wandering Jew; "El informe de Brodie" is supposedly the work of one David Brodie, a fictitious nineteenth-century Scottish missionary; the plot of "Las ruinas circulares" is ascribed to the nonexistent author, Herbert Quain; and *Seis problemas para don Isidro Parodi* is imputed to H. Bustos Domecq, really a golem-writer created by Borges and Adolfo Bioy Casares.

Closely related to these mystifications are the references to invented books and the commentaries on fictitious works which pepper Borges's writings: the list of Pierre Menard's nineteen "visible" volumes; the synopsis of Mir Bahadur Ali's novel, *The Approach to al-Mu'tasim*; or the compendium and "examination" of Herbert Quain's varied works. In this aspect of the pseudepigraphic method, too, Borges may have found a precursor in de León, for as Scholem wrote (and Borges read): "the author [of the *Zohar*] not only fails to indicate his real

---

[20] Alazraqui discusses certain aspects of this subject in "Borges and the Kabbalah," pp. 202–06.

[21] Barrenechea deals with this form of irreality in *Borges, the Labyrinth Maker*, pp. 127ff. See Borges's comments on this subject in "Magias parciales del Quijote," *OC*, 669; and "Avatares de la tortuga," *OC*, 258.

sources but supplies fantastic references to nonexistent ones"
(*Major Trends*, p. 174).

De León carried out his "hoax" (Borges's description for
"al-Mu'tasim") in the name of perpetuating a heritage and,
simultaneously, updating it; Borges executed his deceptions in
the name of questioning reality, of suggesting that if the
author of a work can be a shadow, we, his readers may also be
simulacra in a universe of chance. Yet the concern that mo-
tivated de León's pseudepigraphy—the desire for both innovation and preservation—was not alien to Borges. It was, on
the contrary, an important matter for him. As early as 1926, in
an essay appropriately entitled "La aventura y el orden,"[22]
Borges took up the question of tradition and change, clearly
enunciating the position which was to inform all of his work:
"Grato es el gesto que en una brusca soledad resplandece;
grata es la voz antigua que denuncia nuestra comunidad con
los hombres . . . " (p. 74). Like de León—and unlike many of
his avant-garde contemporaries—Borges recognized and in
large measure accepted the shaping influence of tradition, the
ancient voice that represents continuity with the past. At the
same time, like the Kabbalist, he was aware of the need for the
solitary gesture, the brusque break with history. But if both
disciplines, insolent innovation and decorous preservation,
are accepted, the problem becomes how to forge a coexistence
between the two, how to effect a synthesis between rebellion
and continuity. De León's pseudepigraphy was one solution;
through it, as Biale had written, the authority of tradition is
recognized, but the freedom of literary creativity is preserved.
Borges, however, had chosen not to utilize pseudepigraphy
for that end.[23] What he did, nevertheless, was to use another

---

[22] *El tamaño de mi esperanza*, pp. 70–74. The original version of the essay,
under the title "Sobre un verso de Apollinaire," had appeared in 1925 in
Nosotros, 49, No. 190, 320–22. The verse in question is from Apollinaire's
poem—his manifesto of modernity—"La Jolie Rousse":

Je juge cette longue querelle de la tradition et de l'invention
De l'Ordre de l'Aventure

[23] There is one Borges story where pseudepigraphy does seem to be
used to combine tradition with innovation: "El inmortal." The tale is pre-

of the Spanish Kabbalist's techniques for incorporating even while updating tradition. This technique is textual commentary and interpretation, which is, in essence, the revisionist misreading and rewriting of canonical texts.

The *Zohar*, the representative book of Kabbalism, was not only pseudepigraphal; it was also organized as a commentary on Scripture (*Major Trends*, pp. 157, 171). By presenting itself in this dress, the *Zohar* declared its ties with tradition openly and unequivocally. But the Zoharic gloss was no rehashing of what was already written. De León displayed such "audacious freedom of interpretation" in his book (Biale, p. 99), making his exegesis so daring and innovative, that he effectively "misread" and then "rewrote" much of the canonical text, on occasion even turning the meaning of the ancestral voice into its own opposite (Bloom, p. 34; *Major Trends*, 169).

According to Harold Bloom in *Kabbalah and Criticism*, this Zoharic-kabbalistic methodology, far from being some forgotten *modus operandi*, became the paradigm for Western writers trying to come to terms with their own "overdetermined tradition" (p. 83). These writers, like de León, were confronted with a "massive and completed Scripture" in the form of the works of their illustrious precursors. Such a venerable canon could not be wished or washed away; its burden, its influence had to be coped with consciously or unconsciously. How, then, could fresh and vital impulses be accommodated into the tradition? (p. 33) Through misreading and rewriting, says Bloom; that is, through audacious freedom of interpretation. Bloom remarks that writers

> from the Renaissance through today have sought occult authority in the Kabbalah, but, I suspect that this seeking concealed and

---

sented as the chronicle of Cartaphilus, a composite of the ancient Greek, Homer, and the ancient Wandering Jew, witness to the Crucifixion. These two archetypal figures of Western culture are also the writers of its essential myths: the Odyssey and the Passion. By presenting the story as their work, Borges emphasizes the continuity of tradition. At the same time, his handling of the Homer / Cartaphilus tale is a new interpretation which is given legitimacy by putting it under the pen of the two most hoary and authoritative authors.

conceals a more professional concern. However 'unconsciously' poets seem to have known that their work followed the Kabbalistic model. Not their content nor their form derived from Kabbalistic example, but rather the more crucial matter of their *stance*, their stance towards tradition and towards their precursors. (pp. 90–91)

His comments apply perfectly to Borges, who knows that the Kabbalah stands both for tradition and for the almost heretical belief that Scripture has as many true meanings as readers; whose canonical essay vindicates the hermeneutic procedures used by the mystics to make new ideas seem to derive naturally from the old biblical text;[24] and whose own stance towards tradition, articulated with even greater precision in the 1951 lecture-essay "El escritor argentino y la tradición," sounds much like a modern-day secularized version of the kabbalistic posture.

In that piece, Borges openly and unequivocally declares his acceptance of the Western tradition and its canon. (*OC*, 272). He also suggests that his writing is definitely tied to this canon because it is, above all, a "manipulation" of Western themes—just as the *Zohar* had been a "manipulation" of Scripture. But, Borges continues, accepting and working with tradition do not imply sclerotic repetition; *irreverencia*, audacious freedom of interpretation, is the attitude one must assume in handling the eternal metaphors of the West, the long-lived fables that Borges believes are the substance of every Western writing (*OC*, 273).

Thus, Borges's books often derive from works consecrated by the centuries: The *Iliad* and the Chronicle of the Wandering Jew in "El inmortal";[25] the Bible in "Tres versiones de Judas" and "El evangelio según Marcos"; Greek mythology

---

[24] See "El misticismo judío y las leyendas de la cábala," p. 6; "A Manuel Mujica Lainez," *La moneda de hierro* (Buenos Aires: Emecé, 1976), p. 49; and the introduction to Swedenborg's works, *Prólogos*, p. 157.

[25] The Chronicle of the Wandering Jew is a type of narration developed around the legendary figure, and supposedly authored by him. In it, this Jew, condemned to eternal wandering for having negated and mistreated Jesus, tells of his adventures in different ages and places. See, George K. Anderson, *The Legend of the Wandering Jew* (Providence: Brown University Press, 1965), p. 128.

in "La casa de Asterión" and "There Are More Things"; Cervantes's *Quijote* in "Pierre Menard, autor del Quijote"; Shakespeare's *Macbeth* and *Julius Caesar* in "Tema del traidor y del héroe." Such canonical or classic works, the "scriptures" that Borges interprets, need not be from antiquity or the relatively distant past, however. More recent masterpieces, including those belonging to the Argentine branch of Western civilization, can and do form part of the canon which Borges weaves and unweaves in his writings. The story "El otro," takes up the theme of the double ably presented by Robert Louis Stevenson; "La lotería en Babilonia" and "La biblioteca de Babel" are inspired by Kafka; and "Biografía de Tadeo Isidoro Cruz (1829–74)" is a gloss on Argentina's great book, *Martín Fierro*.

It is precisely with regard to this most canonical of Argentine works that Borges reiterates and expounds on the idea of *irreverencia* in approaching tradition. Borges prologued three editions of the poem by José Hernández,[26] and in each he emphasizes that the author worked within a tradition: gauchesque poetry. Yet no sooner does Borges underline Hernández's ties to tradition than he adds how Hernández did the only thing possible with that tradition: renew and modify it (1962 introduction, p. 95). And that is what Borges, in turn, has done to Hernández. Borges's gloss on *Martín Fierro*, "Biografía de Tadeo Isidoro Cruz (1829–74)," fills in details of Sargent Cruz's life; relates the thoughts and emotions going through the soldier's mind as he comes to Fierro's aid; and develops the theme of the identity of victim and pursuer, a Borges favorite. All these themes are not found in Hernández, but, through Borges's skill, seems to flow naturally from the older book. What Scholem says about the Jewish mystics and *their* canonical text is pertinent here:

A large part of Kabbalistic literature consists in commentary to Biblical books . . . Many of the most creative minds among the

---

[26] These forewords are reprinted in *Prólogos*, pp. 89–99. They, together with other forewords to literary works, and Borges's many essays on literary masterpieces and their creators, must also be seen as part of the view of writing as commentary, interpretation and translation. Borges in fact foreworded or wrote articles about most of the great works he "rewrites."

Kabbalists have found this a most congenial method for conveying their own ideas, and, at the same time, of making these ideas seem to flow, as it were, naturally out of Scripture. It is not always easy to say in a given instance whether Scripture actually gave the impetus to the birth of the exegesis, or whether the exegesis is an artificial creation designed to bridge the gap that frequently opens between an old and a new vision. ("The Meaning of the Torah," p. 37)

With Borges, too, it is hard to say whether *Martín Fierro* in fact stimulated his modifications, or whether his gloss was designed to give expression to a new idea—that all men are the same man—which is given weight and honor by being misread into the canonical work. (Probably, as Scholem suggests with regard to the Kabbalists, the process of rewriting contained a bit of both elements.)

The principle of transformation, modification and renovation of tradition is likewise at work in Borges's other writings. "Tres versiones de Judas" (the word "versions" in the title indicates the process) transforms the time-honored view of Judas as the antithesis of Jesus by presenting Iscariot as a reflection of Christ, then as a facilitator of Jesus's mission, and finally as the true Redeemer Himself; "La casa de Asterión" modifies the myth of the Minotaur, making the fear-inspiring, cannibalistic demigod into a pathetic monstrosity awaiting release from his agony through death;[27] and "Pierre Menard, autor del Quijote" renovates Cervantes's masterpiece by describing its twentieth-century rewriting, a rewriting which, though recounted parodically, suggests in all seriousness that great works become richer, subtler and more complex as they go through the repetitions and perversions of successive ages.

Borges's view of literature as the revisionist glossing of traditional texts, a view which Bloom ultimately traces to a medieval model, the Kabbalah, has become the *dernier cri* in critical thinking about authors and their texts. As Claudia Hoffer Gosselin puts it:

---

[27] See, Rodríguez Monegal, *Biography*, pp. 41–47; Alazraqui, "Borges and the Kabbalah," p. 208.

Recent literary theories posit a writer always operating within an already constituted literary system and thus never completely "original," as well as a text that is no longer a purely passive reflection of preexistent thought but an active, generating mechanism in its own right. The writer is seen as always producing his text within the framework of the texts that have preceded his and that he is always "realizing, transforming or transgressing."[28]

Gosselin's description of recent literary theories, most particularly what is now termed "intertextuality," seems much like a profane restatement of the Kabbalah's literary theory, which is akin to Borges's literary theory. Once again, as in the case of the biblical idea of an impersonal, dictated literature, the Jobian poetics of uncanny facts expressed through uncanny symbols, or the kabbalistic concept of the book as an end in itself, Borges's vindication and desacralization of a hoary religio-esthetic notion is, in effect, the vindication and anticipation of the most up-to-date perspectives in literature.

---

[28] Claudia Hoffer Gosselin, "Voices of the Past in Claude Simon's *La Bataille de Pharsale*," in *Intertextuality*, p. 24.

3. The Diverse Intonation of Some Jewish Metaphors

Introduction

It is a known fact that the word "invention" originally stood for "discovery," and thus the Roman Church celebrates the Invention of the Cross, not its unearthing or discovering. Behind this etymological shift we may, I think, glimpse the whole Platonic doctrine of archetypes—of all things being already there. William Morris thought that the essential stories of man's imagination had long since been told and that by now the storyteller's craft lay in rethinking and retelling them . . . To me the writing of a story has more of discovery about it than of deliberate invention.

Los mitos de Israel . . . nos tocan como una música, como si fuera nuestra íntima voz.[1]

This section will discuss three salient Judaic archetypes in Borges to examine why he uses them, and how they are realized, transformed or transgressed in his works.

---

[1] Jorge Luis Borges, "Afterword," *Doctor Brodie's Report*, trans. Norman Thomas di Giovanni in collaboration with the author (New York: E. P. Dutton, 1971), p. 123; the words about the myths of Israel were part of a short speech given by Borges at a banquet held to celebrate the twenty-fifth anniversary of the Sociedad Hebraica Argentina (3 May 1951). They were recorded in the organization's bulletin, *S.H.A.*, 20, No. 338 (June 1951), 6–7.

The first of these paradigmatic tales is scriptural. Because Borges considers the Bible the place where all things began, his writings give renewed intonation to some of the fundamental accounts found in Holy Writ, among them the Genesis story of Cain and Abel. This primeval narration exerts a powerful pull on Borges, echoing over and over in his texts, and receiving various treatments and interpretations.

But the prototypic Jewish tales that attract Borges are not only biblical. During the course of the Jew's millennial sojourn in Christian Europe, new metaphors came to be associated with him. One of these was the myth of the Jew-as-Brain, what Raphael Patai calls the "rumor" of Jewish intelligence.[2] Derived in part from the association of the Jews with the Bible, and from their subsequent preeminence in the "thinking" professions, this image of the gifted Jewish mind is deeply imbedded in Christendom's consciousness. For Borges, it is perhaps the Jewish Metaphor-of-Metaphors, fed, confirmed and strengthened by his personal and textual contacts with Jews.

Then there is the Argentine scene. Borges may be an "exiled European," but at the most immediate level he is an Argentine.[3] And from his homeland he has likewise drawn a Jewish essential tale he can manipulate: the saga of the Jewish gaucho. An offshoot of the great River Plate myth embodied in Hernández's *Martín Fierro*, this story is also associated with a canonical work: Alberto Gerchunoff's *Los gauchos judíos*. Though Borges recreates the Jewish "cowboy" immortalized by Gerchunoff to a lesser extent and in a more jocular manner than archetypes like Cain and Abel or the Jew-as-Intellect, his handling of it is nonetheless worthy of consideration. The story of the *gaucho judío* is Argentine Jewry's ethnic myth, and by charting Borges's reaction to it, much can be learned about his views on the gaucho and the Jew, as well as on nationalism and universalism—fundamental figures and fundamental

---

[2] Raphael Patai, *The Jewish Mind* (New York: Charles Scribner's Sons, 1977), p. 287.
[3] Borges used this phrase in my interview with him.

issues in his work. Much can also be learned about the ideological factors which influence the manipulation of archetypes by Borges and other writers (Gerchunoff, for example), the reasons why a myth is rethought in one or another way.

A. It's the Story of Cain/Who Continues Killing Abel

A short poem called "Génesis IV, 8," which appeared in Borges 1972 verse collection, *El oro de los tigres*,[1] is a good place to begin the search for answers to the following questions: Why does the scriptural account of Cain, the slayer, and Abel, the slain, fascinate Borges? What aspects of it reverberate in his work? And how does Borges modify the canonical text, rewriting the biblical narration?

This is the way "Génesis IV, 8" reads:

Fue en el primer desierto.
Dos brazos arrojaron una gran piedra.
No hubo un grito. Hubo sangre.
Hubo por vez primera la muerte.
Ya no recuerdo si fui Abel o Caín.
(*OC*, 1092)

What Borges does in these five lines is to gloss the moment in the pentateuchal story when the elder brother, overwhelmed by jealousy and hatred because Abel's offering was accepted by God while his was rejected, sheds the first blood, introducing death into the world. Borges chooses to work with this particular one-verse fragment of the chapter-long account not only because it is one of the dramatic highpoints in the episode, but also because it contains the two aspects of the tale that attract him most: the antagonistic, yet intimately related pair, and the element of violence. In the various Borges texts which reflect the biblical story, these are the facets of the narration inevitably selected for retelling and rethinking. On

---

[1] "Génesis IV, 8" appeared as one of thirteen short poems under the general title, "Trece monedas," *OC*, 1092. It was later included in "Quince monedas," *La rosa profunda* (Buenos Aires: La Ciudad, 1976), n. pag.

the pages of the author's works, Cain and Abel are synonymous with the homicidal stone, the chilling scream of death that wasn't, the spilled life-blood. They are also synonymous with the never-ending, often-mortal confrontation of person against person, a confrontation in which, Borges believes, each person really turns against himself. The Genesis story, with its violent primitivism, its outrage at the useless shedding of blood, and its bipolarity (Cain/Abel) coupled with unity (they are of the same flesh) contained the seeds of ideas to become pivotal in Borges's literature.

One way Borges's work reflects the sanguinariness of Cain and Abel is intimately connected to his Argentine heritage. When asked by María Esther Vázquez to explain why his books are full of daggers, swords, combats, and homicides Borges said that there were two reasons for this: his family history, and his interest in the *compadritos*, the toughs of the Buenos Aires slums (Vázquez,p. 55). Born at the tail end of a century of national strife—independence struggles, Indian wars, internecine fighting—to a family whose members participated actively in these battles, Borges feels that the sword is an inextricable part of his background. That feeling is only reinforced by Argentina's popular mythology which Borges, like most Argentines, has absorbed as part of his ethnic inheritance. In large measure a reflection of the country's sanguinary past, this mythology has as its heroes two macho types quick to the draw of the knife: the gaucho, and his urban counterpart, the *compadrito*.[2] Both have long since disappeared from the Argentine scene, but their heroic—violent—deeds form the backbone of Argentina's folklore, the national mythos preserved and elaborated in poems like *Martín Fierro*, and transmitted from generation to generation. Though Borges realizes full well that his destiny is not to shed blood with the sword, but to create art with the pen, in his literature he expresses nostalgic admiration for the cult of macho bravery that is part of his legacy.

---

[2] Borges discusses these two "vast generic figures" in "Historia del tango," *OC*, 162 ff.

This native tradition of violence which Borges presents in his books must be considered a factor in his fascination with the Cain and Abel story. One of the compositions in which Borges explicitly rewrites the biblical tale is "Milonga de dos hermanos" (*OC*, 955–56). No work could be more stereotypically Argentine: it is written in the form of a milonga—an ancestor of the tango—and has as subject the life and death of two *compadritos*, the Iberra brothers. And yet, Borges insinuates throughout the milonga and states openly in the final couplet, the story of the Iberras—with its envy of the older sibling for the younger and its entrapment and murder of the junior brother by the senior one—is really the story of Cain and Abel:

Velay, señores, la historia
De los hermanos Iberra,
Hombres de amor y de guerra
Y en el peligro primeros,
La flor de los cuchilleros
Y ahora los tapa la tierra.

Suelen al hombre perder
La soberbia o la codicia;
También el coraje envicia
A quien le da noche y día—
El que era menor debía
Más muertes a la justicia.

Cuando Juan Iberra vio
Que el menor lo aventajaba,
La paciencia se le acaba
Y le armó no sé qué lazo—
Le dio muerte de un balazo,
Allá por la Costa Brava. . .

Así de manera fiel
Conté la historia hasta el fin;
Es la historia de Caín
Que sigue matando a Abel.

Borges's linking of the scriptural siblings and the Argentine brothers may, however, be due to more than the common elements of brotherhood, jealousy and murder. For beyond any other brand of Argentine violence it was the *compadrito's* and gaucho's kind that could be connected to the biblical narration. As the milonga indicates, such violence was typified by the personalized one-to-one assault in the clearing, plain or desert, on the fringe of civilization, most frequently using a rudimentary weapon. Its distant forerunner thus seemed to be the skirmish between Cain and Abel, the primeval adversaries, locked in a struggle to the death in the first wilderness, using the simplest of arms.

That is probably why in the Borges stories that take up the theme of native violence, stories like "Biografía de Tadeo Isidoro Cruz (1829–1874)," "El fin" and "El Sur," the portrayal of the setting, the antagonists and the fighting is evocative of the atmosphere, opponents and assault in the Cain and Abel tale (or Borges's elaboration of the Cain and Abel tale). All three occur on the *llanura*, the Argentine plain, an elemental zone much like the world of the biblical brothers. This wilderness is the backdrop for the blood-tinged, Cain and Abel-like confrontation between Martín Fierro and the black man, between Juan Dahlmann and the gaucho, and between Fierro and Cruz. The weapons used are similarly primitive and reminiscent of the archetypal rock: the *facón*, or large gaucho knife. In his "Historias de jinetes," Borges directly indicates the association between the wasteland of the scriptural siblings and Cruz and Fierro's land when he mentions the gaucho and the shepherd Abel as two examples of the savage nomad, men of the wide spaces and emblems of an epic primitivism (*OC*, 152–55).

On the pages of the same essay, however, Borges intimates that the animosity between Cain and Abel interests him for more than local reasons. It attracts him too, he implies, as a symbol of the ongoing strife between people: "Los centauros vencidos por los lapitas, la muerte del pastor de ovejas Abel a manos de Caín, que era labrador, la derrota de la caballería de Napoleón por la infantería británica en Waterloo" (*OC*, 154). When Borges speaks in a poem of "la incestuosa guerra/De Caínes y Abeles y su cría," he makes clear by the plural form of the brothers' names and by the word "progeny" that all shedding of one person's blood by another is a replay of the initial homicide ("Adam Cast Forth, *OC*, 934). The composition where Borges enunciates this idea most forcefully is "In

113

Memoriam J.F.K.," where he traces the geneology of the bullet that killed President Kennedy through the centuries back to the stone that at the dawn of time Cain hurled against Abel (*OC*, 853).

In the piece there is none of the romanticizing backward glance that was part of Borges's Argentine retelling of the biblical episode. There, the horror of the story of Cain who kills Abel (which is the essence of the scriptural original) had been tempered by the patina of time, by the nostalgic and glorifying remembrance of things past. But in the very real and violent present which Borges was living, no such glorification was possible. Cain's stone hurled against Abel could only be portrayed as the perennial weapon of destruction, ultimately threatening to do away with humanity itself. (*OC*, 853).

In connecting Cain's violence to the incessant bloodshed throughout history, and particularly to the extinction of humankind, Borges is echoing a normative Jewish interpretation of the Genesis episode, which he himself cites. The reference appears in "Nueva refutación del tiempo":

> El quinto párrafo del cuarto capítulo del tratado *Sanhedrín* de la Mishnah declara que, para la Justicia de Dios, el que mata a un solo hombre, destruye el mundo; si no hay pluralidad, el que aniquilara a todos los hombres no sería más culpable que el primitivo y solitario Caín, lo cual es ortodoxo, ni más universal en la destrucción, lo que puede ser mágico. Yo entiendo que así es. (*OC*, 763)

The source Borges quotes from, the body of Jewish law and scriptural commentary known as the Mishnah, glosses Cain's murder of Abel in two ways. It affirms that the odious strife between the brothers reverberates in their offspring; and it suggests that he who, like Cain, destroys one life in fact destroys the whole world because each individual is a microcosm, the universe condensed.

By reading the pentateuchal fratricide as a condemnation of the eternal, species-threatening nature of violence, Borges moves closest to the "orthodox" intent of the scriptural original. (He himself intimates so.) This intent, mirrored in the Mishnaic interpretation, was to teach that the "crime of murder is inexpressibly terrible" and that a world where blood-

114

shed prevails is "hateful."[3] In the poem "El," Borges again empasizes his identification with this aim of the Bible episode when he has the homicidal elder brother (who is the speaker in the work) say:

Me llamaban Caín. Por mí el Eterno
Sabe el sabor del fuego del infierno.

(OC, 898)

Through Cain the killer, the cosmos—the sum of the attributes of the Eternal, as Borges implies elsewhere in the poem—can only become a chaos, a living hell.

But Borges's interest in the Mishnaic commentary is due to more than antipathy towards senseless slaughter. What calls his attention, too, is the interplay of individuality and plurality which is the essence of the gloss. This theme of multiplicity and singularity, and its variation, duality and identity, is basic in Borges, as he himself has pointed out.[4] He discovers this theme in the Mishnaic commentary on Cain and Abel, and also finds it suggested in the original narrative, where the interplay of twoness/oneness, discord/harmony, Cain and Abel as antagonists and, simultaneously, as of the same flesh, is all-important. Borges makes his attraction to this aspect of the biblical account clear in "Génesis IV, 8," when he writes "I no longer remember if I was Abel or Cain," and also in "Leyenda," another of his glosses on the biblical story:

Abel y Caín se encontraron después de la muerte de Abel. Camina-ban por el desierto y se reconocieron de lejos, porque los dos eran muy altos. Los hermanos se sentaron en la tierra, hicieron un fuego y comieron. Guardaban silencio, a la manera de la gente cansada cuando declina el día. En el cielo asomaba alguna estrella que aún no había recibido su nombre. A la luz de las llamas, Caín advirtió en la frente de Abel la marca de la piedra y dejó caer el pan que estaba por llevarse a la boca y pidió que le fuera perdonado su crimen. Abel contestó: —¿Tú me has matado o yo te he matado? Ya no recuerdo; aquí estamos juntos como antes.

(OC, 1013)

---

[3] Umberto Cassuto, *A Commentary on the Book of Genesis*, trans. Israel Abrahams (Jerusalem: The Magnes Press, 1961), pp. 184, 244.

[4] See his comments in *The Aleph and Other Stories*, p. 277.

In this text the interaction of discord and harmony or, more precisely, of discord resolved in harmony, is quite apparent. On the one hand, the shadow of the otherness, the breach between the brothers hangs over Borges's legend: their meeting is after Abel's murder; Abel carries the scar of his mortal wound; Cain alludes to his crime; Abel refers to it as well. On the other hand, the sameness of the rivals is continually emphasized: their consanguinity is not only recalled by the fact that they are brothers, but also by their similar height; the mark on Abel's forehead is the mirror-image of the proverbial mark of Cain, the sign of infamy and protection placed by God on the killer's brow;[5] and, most importantly, as in "Génesis IV, 8," the distinction between slayer and slain has been blurred: Abel and Cain are each both murderer and murdered, having come together into one not so much through the bond of life as through the shared destiny of death.

This Borgesian rendering of the Cain and Abel story realizes Scripture and also transgresses it. In the canonical account the breach between the siblings is emphasized; so is their closeness. (One commentator points out the insistent repetition of the word "brother," which appears six times in just two verses [Genesis IV: 8–10].[6]) The whole narrative is, in fact, organized around the dual axes of antagonism and attachment. Borges retains this orthodox polarity. But his orthodoxy is overwhelmed by heterodoxy when he stretches the brothers' attachment—against the grain of Scripture—to the point of indifferentiation. In the Bible there is no such (con)fusion of personalities or actions. Cain and Abel, good and evil, reward and punishment stand in sharp contrast on the pages of Genesis. The unequivocal distinction between the siblings, their behavior and their fate stems from the purpose of Scripture in telling the story, which is to teach "that God calls [each] man to account, awakening him according to his works" (Cassuto, p. 184). The closeness of the brothers is reiterated not to show

[5] Though the scriptural original says nothing about the place of the sign, a common tradition has it that it was on Cain's forehead.
[6] Nahum M. Sarna, *Understanding Genesis* (New York: The Jewish Theological Seminary of America and McGraw-Hill, 1966), p. 30.

that they are indistinguishable, but to underscore the heinous-
ness of Cain's crime and the magnitude of his *personal* burden.
In the Borges version the central point in the Genesis narration
is transgressed because the writer's aims in retelling the story
are different from those of Scripture. Among these the desire
to produce amazement in the reader should not be over-
looked. By perverting the time-honored associations Cain
equals villain/Abel equals hero, he provokes such astonish-
ment and wonder. It is in this provocation of strangeness in
the most familiar, to paraphrase Saúl Yurkievich, that much of
Borges's originality as a writer lies.[7]

Yet strangeness is not all there is to Borges's transgression of Scripture. Genesis had portrayed the brothers as close
but not confounded because it was most interested in them as
individuals, each with his own singular destiny (slayer/slain);
Borges, on the other hand, allows them to reverse roles and
lets the distinction between them lapse because he is more
concerned with them as nonindividuals, sharers of a common
and interchangeable fate. Fully aware that every individual is
constrained by her particular life situation and by her unique—
tragic—destiny, Borges has made the elimination of such con-
straints the essence of his literary creed. He believes that by
removing the limitations of personal circumstance in the world
of fiction, he and his readers can better cope with them in the
world of fact. As he puts it: "I suppose that the function of
literature is to serve as a sort of dream for Man, perhaps
helping him thereby to live in reality."[8] To achieve that aim
Borges appropriates various folkloric and literary traditions,
and several philosophico-religious tendencies, which imply
such a nullification.[9] One of these is the topos of the identification of slayer and slain. In his rewriting of the Cain and Abel
story it is this theme that Borges grafts onto the biblical trunk,

[7] Saúl Yurkievich, *Fundadores de la nueva poesía latinoamericana* (Barcelona:
Barral, 1970), p. 137. See Borges's comments on the subject in the prologue to
El informe de Brodie, OC, 1022.

[8] Barrenechea, *Borges, the Labyrinth Maker*, p. 151. See also, the introduction to Ralph Waldo Emerson's *Hombres representativos*, *Prólogos*, p. 38.

[9] See *Borges, the Labyrinth Maker*, pp. 87–97.

which seems ready to receive it by providing the consangineous murderer and murdered.

In this grafted form the essential tale from Scripture is available to Borges's readers as "Génesis IV, 8" and "Leyenda," the two texts which most explicitly hark back to the scriptural archetype; but it can also be discerned in a narration like "Los teólogos" (*OC*, 550–556), singled out by Borges as an illustration of his concern with identity and its discord, duality (*The Aleph and Other Stories*, p. 277).

In the theological fiction, the outlines of the Cain and Abel episode according to Borges are quite distinct. There is an antagonistic, but intimately related pair, the rival theologians Aureliano de Aquilea and Juan de Panonia. Although they are brothers in Christ, united by their shared preoccupation with defending the faith, they are separated by Aureliano's jealousy towards Juan. This jealousy stems from the acceptance of Juan's "offering," a refutation of an heretical sect, by God's representatives, the Church authorities in Rome, and the rejection of Aureliano's parallel "oblation." As in the Genesis account, the spurned member of the pair brings about his companion's death, only to suffer a similar fate and be merged with him in the afterlife.

That "Los teólogos" retells the story of the biblical fratricide as understood by Borges seems clear from the points of contact cited above. But imbedded in the story there is an additional clue which also indicates a link between Borges's Cain and Abel and his Aureliano and Juan. In fact, this clue not only strengthens the connection between the scriptural siblings and the theological duad; it also points to another tradition which, along with the topos of accuser-victim, was appropriated by Borges for his personality-blurring rewriting of the Genesis tale. The clue is the word *cainitas* (*OC*, 552), one of the names of the heretical sect Aureliano is bent on destroying, and the tradition is Gnosticism.[10]

---

[10] The Gnostic tradition has always interested Borges. The 1932 essay, "Una vindicación del falso Basílides," *OC*, 213–16, indicates that his interest in Gnosticism dates from the very outset of his career. In the essay, Borges

The Cainites, a Gnostic school which in fact existed,[11] gave a particular twist to the system of antitheses—highest God/Demiurge, earthly man/spiritual man, good/evil— typical to Gnosticism. Of the possible oppositions available to them, the Cainites chose to focus on the one which pitted Cain against Abel, proposing a value reversal that made Cain the superior brother and Abel the inferior. (The same transposition was applied to the Judas/Jesus pair.[12]) What the Cainites did, in other words, was to take the Bible's antagonistic, yet intimately-related duad and confound the scriptural line of demarcation between them. The purpose of this confounding was an ultimate unity, the reintegration of fallen, earthly man with his divine, ideal counterpart. Such a restoration of man with his splintered self could only come about by going through all human experiences, by giving even infamy—that inextricable part of terrestrial existence—its due in order to become liberated from it and thus attain wholeness, salvation.[13] The Cainite-Gnostic doctrine, then, not only blurred or overturned the biblical distinction between Cain and Abel; it did so in the name of a final oneness, a coming together of man's divided being. In "Los teólogos," Borges echoes these Cainite-Gnostic doctrines when he writes that the sectarians

imaginaron que todo hombre es dos hombres y que el verdadero es el otro, que está en el cielo...Muertos, nos uniremos a él y seremos

mentions some of the books he read on the subject, among them studies by Mead, Schultz and Bousset. Bousset and another scholar of Gnosticism, Harnack, are also alluded to in "Los teólogos" (OC, 552). The whole story, in fact, is based on Borges's readings in Gnosticism: the various sects and doctrines he cites recall the Gnostic schools and their teachings, while the controversies between orthodox and heterodox theologians reflect the struggle between Christianity and Gnosticism.

[11] See G. R. S. Mead, *Fragments of a Faith Forgotten* (London: Theosophical Publishing Society, 1900; rpt. with an introd. by Kenneth Rexroth, New York: University Books, 1960), pp. 224–29; and Hans Jonas, *The Gnostic Religion*, 2nd ed. (Boston: Beacon Press, 1963), pp. 95, 273–74.

[12] Another Borges story, "Tres versiones de Judas," OC, 514–18, is based on this Cainite Jesus/Judas inversion. Hans Jonas discusses the subject in "Delimitation of the Gnostic Phenomenon—Typological and Historical," in *The Origins of Gnosticism*, ed. Ugo Bianchi (Leiden: E. J. Brill, 1967), p. 102.

[13] On sin as a way to salvation and unity, consult *The Gnostic Religion*, pp. 59, 273–74.

él...analógicamente, buscaron la purificación por el mal. Entendieron, como Carpócrates, que nadie saldrá de la cárcel [this world] hasta pagar el último óbolo [he has committed every deed there is in this world].

(OC, 553–54)

The Gnostic inversion of Cain and Abel with its intimation of an ultimate unity; the traditional theme of the identification of executed and executioner; and the original Genesis account of the first murder are the major components in Borges's retelling of the Cain and Abel story, a retelling which is fundamental in many of his narrations. Among them are "Tres versiones de Judas," "La secta de los treinta," "El fin," "El duelo," and "Deutsches Requiem." Each revolves around kindred contenders who are in the end confounded or fused through death: Judas "reflects" Jesus and merges with him as a consequence of their common sacrifice (crucifixion/hanging) (*OC*, 515); the black mirrors his adversary, Martín Fierro, and becomes Fierro at the moment he slays the renowned gaucho (*OC*, 521); the rival artists Clara Glencairn and Marta Pizarro paint against and in some way for each other, and are united in a common artistic death when Clara passes away (*OC*, 1057); even zur Linde, the Nazi Jew-hater, and Jerusalem, the Jew, are somehow coalesced through killing, since by condemning the Jew the Nazi in fact condemns himself (*OC*, 580). [14]

In this ongoing production of versions and perversions of the pentateuchal story, Borges puts into practice the kabbalistic-intertextual literary philosophy which he had enunciated in a poetic reference to Luria, the great Jewish mystic, and which Jenny echoes in secularized form in his study on intertextuality:

Isaac Luria declara que la eterna Escritura
Tiene tantos sentidos como lectores. Cada versión es verdadera.

("A Manuel Mujica Lainez," La moneda de hierro, p. 49)

---

[14] Alazraqui in his *Versiones*, studies a complementary source for the author's many stories which revolve (thematically and structurally) around a duality resolved in unity: his well-documented fascination with mirrors.

> ...le livre n'est qu'un système de variantes sans qu'on puisse jamais s'appuyer sur une version "authentique" de l'historiette narrée.
>
> ("La Stratégie de la forme," p. 281)

Scripture, the Cain and Abel episode, is not a congealed text with a single, authentic meaning. Rather, it is a system of variants, with as many readings as readers, each of them true. In line with this audacious freedom of interpretation, the ancestral voices embodied in the canonical book can even be turned into their own opposites (Bloom, *Kabbalah and Criticism*, p. 34). The story of Cain and Abel can be part of a nostalgia for "ignorant knives/and old-time courage" ("A Manuel Mujica Lainez," p. 49); and the unequivocal pentateuchal distinction between murderer and murdered can be blurred in the interest of a literature that frees people from the limitations of personality and circumstance.

But radical as it may be, the rethinking of the sacred stories and the venerable mythologies is, in the final analysis, a strategy to rescue them from ossification, to make them generate new meanings in a continuous process of deconstruction and reconstruction.[15] By glossing the Cain and Abel story with bold irreverence, Borges allows the old biblical tale to have updated pertinence. At the same time, even as he handles the canonical tale with daring freedom in an effort to make it speak to the here and now, he realizes that his very manipulating of the "ancient voice" creates a sense of continuity and permanence in an age most characterized by instability and change.[16]

---

[15] Jean Weisgerber in "The Uses of Quotations in Recent Literature," *Comparative Literature*, 22, No. 1 (Winter, 1970), 36–45, writes, quoting Renato Poggioli, that this dynamic view of tradition—the kabbalistic and modern view—conceives of it "not as a museum but as an atelier, as a continuous process of formation, a constant recreation of new values, a crucible of new experiences" (p. 44).

[16] "La Aventura y el Orden," p. 74. At the end of this discussion of the Cain and Abel archetype, I would like to point out that there is often a hierarchy of archetypes in Borges's tales. That is, while the Cain and Abel story also underlies some of the narrations which I will analyze in the next two chapters it is displaced in importance by other, more immediate and pertinent myths (the myth of the intellectual Jew or of the gaucho). Deploying this hierarchy, I will concentrate in the following pages on these other archetypes.

B. A Man Who Is the Book, . . . the Jew

The Jew-as-Intellect is among the most important Jewish metaphors in Borges. An examination of his works reveals that in large measure, the Jew is for him the Book, the life of the mind incarnate. In making the Jew the archetypal intellect on the pages of his books, Borges once again rethinks a commonplace of Western culture: the belief in "a particularly fortunate intellectual endowment . . . in the . . . Chosen People" (Veblen, p. 470).[1] It is this belief that Thorstein Veblen deals with in the essay so greatly admired by Borges, an essay he mentions frequently in relation to Jews.

Borges's writings contain echoes of other common images related to the Jewish people. For example, in the poem "Israel," where Borges calls the Jew "a man who is the Book," he also recalls that he is "a man condemned to be Shylock." This stereotyped picture of the usurious Jew, probably more imbedded in the Western consciousness than that of the intellectual Jew, is known to Borges, but interests him little. Aside from the reference in "Israel," it is mentioned briefly in "Deutsches Requiem," and forms the archetypal underpinnings for just one of Borges's Jewish characters: Aarón Loewenthal, the avaricious adversary of Emma Zunz.

In contrast, Borges's fascination with the Jew-as-Intellect is strong and reiterated. There are a number of reasons for this preference. To Borges, mental virtues and spiritual labyrinths are all-important. His world is the Library and his priesthood, belles-lettres. The image of the Jew dedicated "to the mission of thinking and writing," would thus engage him to a greater degree than that of the Jew condemned to be a usurer.[2] Furthermore, Borges believes that the Jew exercising his intel-

---

[1] See on the subject, Raphael Patai, *The Jewish Mind*, pp. 287–371; and George Eaton Simpson and J. Milton Yinger, *Racial and Cultural Minorities: An Analysis of Prejudice and Discrimination*, 4th ed. (New York: Harper and Row, 1972), pp. 145–46.

[2] The description comes from Borges's lecture, "Baruch Spinoza," printed in *Conferencias*, pp. 103–12. Borges's characterization appears on p. 104.

ligence is the primary configuration of the Jew, taking precedence over any other. As a member of the ur-civilization of the Occident, the purveyor of the West's essential Text and the world-view that flows from it, the Jew is above all the archetypal man of culture. This image is only reinforced in Borges's mind by the continued contributions of Jews to European civilization, be it in the form of mystical speculation, philosophy or literature. Finally, because he is a wanderer in the labyrinths of the Western spirit, a spirit so molded and influenced by the mind of Israel, the Jew-as-Intellect is the one Borges knows best. His relations with Jews have by and large been with men of letters whom he got to know through their books or through personal contact. This also helps explain why of the possible archetypes available to him Borges prefers the one Veblen called the "intellectually gifted Jew" (p. 475).

In Borges's poems the postbiblical Jew frequently appears in the garb of writer or thinker, usually as one of the intellectuals—Heine, Cansinos-Asséns, Kafka, Spinoza—who had a major role in shaping his identification of the Jew with the mind.[3] But it is in the stories that this figure is more fully developed, again evoking not only the generic image, but the person, world or works of some of the particular intellectuals who impressed Borges most.

The Borges story of the Jewish mind *par excellence* is "El milagro secreto." In it, the author uses a confrontation between the Jewish intellect and the Hitlerlite bullet to give narrative substance to one of the central premises of his literature: that mind can win over matter, that despite its shortcomings the creative intellect is the best means for overcoming time, physical suffering and other limitations of the human condition.[4] Published in 1943, "El milagro secreto" fictional-

---

[3] See his poems on Heine, "Paris, 1856"; on Cansinos-Asséns, "Rafael Cansinos-Asséns" and "A Rafael Cansinos-Asséns"; on Kafka, "Ein Traum," *La moneda de hierro*, p. 131; and on Spinoza, "Spinoza," *OC*, 930, and "Baruch Spinoza," *La moneda de hierro*, p. 119.

[4] See on this, Barrenechea, *Borges, the Labyrinth Maker*, p. 145; and George R. McMurray, *Jorge Luis Borges* (New York: Frederick Ungar, 1980), p. 4.

izes this major Borgesian idea by telling the story of Jaromir Hladík, a German-language Jewish writer from Prague who faces, stays and symbolically defeats the precise and punctual Nazi slaughter machine through the power of his imagination. Although Borges suggests that the inventive spirit constitutes humanity's greatest, if imperfect weapon against an afflicting reality in various ways throughout his writings, his choice of a Jewish form of fabulation for "El milagro secreto" is significant and far from incidental. He wrote the story—considered among his masterpieces—at the height of the Hitlerite onslaught on Judaism and its hybrid-child, Western civilization. This was a period when no one more than the Nazis incarnated brute matter and an infernal existence for the author, and no one more than the Jews—already identified in his mind with culture-making—epitomized intellect and spirituality. In an article written during the World War II years, Borges declared:

> Para los europeos y americanos hay un orden—un solo orden posible: . . . la cultura de Occidente. Ser nazi . . . es, a la larga, una imposibilidad mental y moral. El nazismo . . . es inhabitable; los hombres sólo pueden morir por él, mentir por él, matar y ensangrentar por él. Nadie, en la soledad central de su yo, puede anhelar que triunfe.[5]

The dichotomy Borges delineates here is clear-cut: on the one hand stands the Judaically-inspired culture of the Occident with which are aligned the virtues of the mind and the laws of morality; on the other, an inhabitable Nazi hell of mental and moral vacuity and brute force. In "El milagro secreto," Jaromir Hladík, Jewish of blood, but, more importantly, Jewish of intellect (he is a writer, and the author of "Judaizing" works [OC, 508]), personifies the first side; Julius Rothe, the Gestapo chief, and his cohorts, the second.[6] Ar-

---

[5] "Anotación al 23 de agosto de 1944," pp. 25–26. The essay is collected in the OC, 727–28.

[6] Borges's choice of name for the Gestapo chief is significant. In his essay, "La duración del infierno," he mentions the Evangelical theologian Rothe, who speculated on the meaning and nature of hell (OC, 235–38). Borges writes that Rothe came to the conclusion that the demons, who are enemies of God and His kingdom, are organized into their own diabolic kingdom, for

rested by Rothe's soldiers and condemned to die within days before a Nazi firing squad, Hladík asks God for a "miracle," a year in which to finish his life's task, the drama "Los enemigos." Only through the completion of this intellectual project, the Jewish playwright tells the Lord, can his existence have any meaning. Hladík's request is granted by God in a magical and dramatic way. Just as the German guns converge on the writer, the physical universe—the realm in which the Nazis dominate—comes to a halt. At that moment the universe of the mind—the area of Jewish primacy—expands. God performs a secret miracle for Hladík: the Germans would kill him at the appointed hour, but in his mind a year would pass between the order to fire and the actual firing. During this mental year, Hladík mentally completes his play, a mental creation. Only after he does so, when his life has justification and it no longer really matters, can the Nazi guns kill him—or rather his body, his physical outer shell.

"El milagro secreto," then, is a story about the "miracle" of mind over matter, which is also a reaffirmation of Western culture, and a celebration of the Jewish intellect. In celebrating this intellect, Borges overturns the Hitlerite reading of the Jew-as-Mind, described in this way by Frederic V. Grunfeld:

> In the prevailing mindless frenzy to follow-the-*Führer*, the mere possession of intellect became grounds for suspicion, and "Aryans" who persisted in trying to exercise it were denounced in the Nazi press as *weisse Juden* (white Jews). As one popular Nazi jingle expressed it:
>
> *Intellektueller, du Wort mit dem jüdisch grellen Schein,*
> *Ein rechter deutscher Mann kann nie ein Intellektueller sein!*
>
> Intellectual—the word sounds so Jewish and shrill;
> A true German man can never be an intellectual![7]

For Borges, as for the Nazis, *Intellektueller* meant *Jude*. But

which they elect a head. This head—the Devil—is not one, unchanging figure, but is continually reincarnated in various individuals. The Nazi Julius Rothe, one of the chiefs of the Gestapo, is clearly the latest in the line (*OC*, 508).

[7] Frederic V. Grunfeld, *Prophets Without Honour: A Background to Freud, Kafka, Einstein and Their World* (New York and Philadelphia: Holt, Rinehart and Winston and The Jewish Publication Society of America, 1979), p. 31.

while Hitler's hordes were bent on the annihilation of the German-speaking Jewish and "white Jewish" intelligentsia which had effected a cultural renaissance in the period between the two world wars, Borges was pledged to its acclamation. Though a tribute to the Jewish mind in general, "El milagro secreto" especially salutes the German-Jewish mind, the one that contributed so much to Borges's view of the Jew-as-Intellect, and the one whose creations the Nazis smashed and burnt with particular vehemence.

There are multiple clues built into Borges's story which indicate that "El milagro secreto" is in fact such a salute. Its setting, Prague, is one of these, perhaps the most important. The city by the Moldau is for Borges first and foremost the habitat of the golem, the homunculus of kabbalistic legend whom he initially met through and inevitably associates with a German-language work, Gustav Meyrink's, *Der Golem*. Meyrink, a native of Vienna who spent part of his life in Prague, was not Jewish. But Borges, in an interview, calls him a Jew and mentions him alongside the dean of Judeo-German authors, Heine.[8] Thus Meyrink, through the novel steeped in the lore of the Prague ghetto, became part of that German-Jewish cultural world for Borges. By placing Hladík in the Moldavian milieu of Meyrink's homunculus, and further making him the translator into German of the *Sepher Yezirah*, the kabbalistic treatise on the letters of the Hebrew alphabet and their creative power which was central to the formation of a golem, Borges pays tribute to that world, fast disappearing under the Nazi truncheon.[9]

---

[8] Personal interview. On the association of the golem, Prague and Meyrink, see, also, "Guayaquil," *OC*, 1066.

[9] Borges alludes to the *Sepher Yezirah* and its relation to golem-making in his lecture on "El misticismo judío y las leyendas de la cábala," p. 7. In my interview with him, he suggested one important meaning of the golem symbol for him: the work of art is to its maker, the writer, as the golem is to his creator, the Kabbalist or rabbi: a creation that can never attain perfection, "a failure, really."

The Prague setting of "El milagro secreto" hints at the world of the German-Jewish intellectual in other ways. Hladík, Borges's fictional author, has a very factual address; an apartment on the Zeltnergasse (*OC*, 508). Borges is so specific about Hladík's place of residence because it is where Franz Kafka, one of the greatest of the Jewish intellectuals writing in German, a man whose work Borges calls "singular," lived. It is very likely that Borges found this detail in yet another product of the Prague German-Jewish mind which he knew well: the 1937 biography of the author of "Die Verwandlung" by his close friend and executor, the author Max Brod.[10] In having Hladík reside and write in Kafka's apartment, an apartment Borges probably learned about through Brod, the creator of "El milagro secreto" renders homage to both writers, particularly to Kafka.

The tribute to Kafka, whose "laconic nightmares"—fantasies of conduct and circumstance conveyed in a colorless, compressed style—became a model for Borges's own fictions, is clear not only from the reference to the Zeltnergasse.[11] Hladík's uncanny situation, his impossibility, is a breakdown of chronological time not unrelated to the Kafkan motif of postponement. Like Kafka's hero, he undergoes a hellish *Prozess*—Borges pointedly uses the word *proceso* (*OC*, 509)—in a dream-like, dream-filled atmosphere, and dies at the end. And like Kafka, his major work is a nightmare with no forward movement: the play "Los enemigos," which Borges describes as a "circular delirium" (*OC*, 510).[12]

---

[10] Borges describes Kafka as a unique writer in his introduction to *La metamorfosis* (Buenos Aires: Losada, 1943; rptd. 1965), p. 11; Brod's book, *Franz Kafka: Eine Biographie* (Prague: Heinr. Mercy Sohn, 1937), is cited in "Libros y autores extranjeros," *El Hogar*, 8 July 1938, p. 28.

[11] Borges uses this phrase to describe Kafka's writings in the introd. to *La metamorfosis*, p. 9.

[12] I discuss the impact of Kafka on Borges further in my study, "Kafka, Borges and Contemporary Latin-American Literature, *Newsletter of the Kafka Society of America*, 6, Nos. 1–2 (June–Dec. 1982), 4–13. Other studies on the subject are Margaret Boyd Boegeman, "Paradox Gained: Kafka's Reception in English from 1930 to 1949 and His Influence on the Early Fiction of Borges,

Hladík's drama also alludes to a related element in German cultural life identified by Borges with Judaism: the Expressionist movement. "Los enemigos" is a play of purely Expressionist cut in which "the entire stage becomes the universe of the mind" and time is not chronological, but a function of emotional states.[13] The work's purposeful unreality—Hladík intentionally writes it in verse to remind the spectators that unreality is a necessary condition of art (*OC*, 510)—is a quality of Expressionism that strongly impacted on Borges; his review of the Expressionist Fritz von Unruh's dramatic poem, "Vor der Entscheidung," lays this bare in just a few sentences: "El protagonista es un ulano; entre los otros personajes figura un muerto, un sacerdote, una mujer y el fantasma de Shakespeare. Esa deliberada irrealidad es típica de Unruh" (Libros y autores extranjeros," *El Hogar*, 17 Sept. 1937, p. 24).

In addition to "Los enemigos," Hladík is the author of a series of Expressionist poems which appeared in a 1924 anthology (*OC*, 510). This was about the time Borges published translations of Expressionist poetry as well as his own verses in the Expressionist mode.[14] In the essay "Acerca del expresionismo" (collected in the 1925 *Inquisiciones*), Borges discusses the essence of Expressionist poetic style—the daring, concrete visual images—which he reproduced in his early poems, and which was ascribed to the Expressionists' Judaism. In contrast to the typically abstract, contemplative Ger-

---

Beckett and Nabokov," Diss. University of California (Los Angeles), 1977; and Ben Belitt, "The Enigmatic Predicament: Some Parables of Kafka and Borges," *Prose for Borges*, ed. Charles Newman and Mary Kinzie, pp. 212–37.

[13] Walter H. Sokel, *The Writer in Extremis: Expressionism in Twentieth-Century German Literature* (Stanford: Stanford University Press, 1959), pp. 39 and 41.

[14] In our conversation, Borges told me that he was a subscriber to the two major German Expressionist journals, *Der Sturm* and *Die Aktion*. He noted that the others "isms" were "sheer nonsense, but Expressionism wasn't. It had a mystical background, a political background." On Borges's interest in the movement, see, also, Gloria Videla, "Presencia americana en el ultraísmo español," *Revista de literatura argentina e iberoamericana*, 3, No. 3 (1961), 23.

man lyric, Borges says in the essay, the Expressionists returned to the biblical-Oriental tradition of direct, sensual metaphors (p. 150). In this sense their poetry is a "Judaizing" element in German literature, which was reinforced—and criticized by the "patriotic" anti-Semites (p. 148)—by the fact that many of the Expressionists were Jews.

"El milagro secreto" is thus an Aleph—the Hebrew symbol is appropriate to the Judaic context—a microcosm that miniaturizes the vibrant Jewish-German intellectual macrocosm of pre-Hitler days. And, despite the Nazi Final Solution, Borges's miniaturization is not a swan song but an affirmation of continued life. By the very act of writing "El milagro secreto" and weaving into it so many threads from the world of the *jüdischer Intellektueller*, the author asserts that Meyrink and his homunculus along with Kafka, Brod and their Jewish-German Expressionist fellows live on—through Borges.

The same attitude towards the German-Jewish intellect is expressed in another story from the Holocaust era, the 1946 "Deutsches Requiem" (*OC*, 576–581). Here, as in "El milagro secreto," the narration is anchored in a confrontation between the Jewish mind and the Nazi bullet, with each side represented by an emblematic character: Otto Dietrich zur Linde, a Nazi concentration camp subcommandant, standard-bearer of the faith of the sword; and his victim, David Jerusalem, a famous German-Jewish poet, symbol of the many Jewish intellectuals tortured and killed by the Third Reich (*OC*, 580; 579). In the story Borges contrasts the degrading treatment Jerusalem receives as a Jew under Nazism with his poetic genius, a genius used to celebrate the joys of life (*OC*, 578). Zur Linde, the New Man, the Man of Iron (whom Borges, with devastating irony makes a one-legged cripple) explains that he must be severe with Jerusalem, allowing neither his intellectual glory nor a sense of compassion to get in the way, because the poet had become a hated part of his own soul (*OC*, 579). The "part" he is referring to is clear from his words and the rest of the story: it is the Judaically-associated realm of mind and morality; it is the Western civilization which first went forth out of Jerusalem and continues in men like David Jerusalem;[15] it is also German culture, whose literary language is rooted in the work of Luther, translator of the Bible, and whose most noted poet was a precursor of Jerusalem's, Heinrich Heine. Zur Linde, a German, a man of the West, and hence a "Jew" (this explains why he and Jerusalem are really one), knows full well that to become the Nazis' New Man this inextricable part of his soul must be expunged at all cost: whatever has to be destroyed will be in order to rid the world of Judaism and its "sickness," Christianity, and to establish the rule of the strong (*OC*, 580–81).

In "Deutsches Requiem" Borges recalls that one way the Nazis expunged the Jewish intellect and its derivates from the New Germany was physical: Jerusalem commits suicide in the concentration camp after being tortured (*OC*, 579). But Borges also alludes to another method employed by the Reich to separate the Judaic intellectual "chaff" from the "wheat" of German nationhood: the rewriting of Germany's history so as to exclude any reference to the *jüdischer Intellektueller* and his "white Jewish" brethren. When zur Linde recounts his lineage and the worthy deeds of the men in his family, he mentions only his military ancestors, omitting the name of his most renowned, intellectual, "Jewish" forebear, the theologian and Hebraist, Johannes Forkel (*OC*, 576). While the omission has shades of the Nazis' witch hunting for Jewish ancestors, which Borges found ridiculous, it is also reminiscent of the type of censorship which irked him even more. As he put it in an article:

El doctor Johannes Rohr (de Berlín) ha revisado, renovado y ger-

---

[15] During our talk Borges also revealed that the name Jerusalem is connected to Karl Wilhelm Jerusalem, an acquaintance of Goethe's whose suicide over an unhappy love affair was a major inspiration for *Werther*. David Jerusalem, who also commits suicide, is thus an homage to Goethe, the prototype of ecumenical understanding, as Borges writes in the story (*OC*, 577). Goethe, in other words, is a representative of the cultured, open Germany, not of the barbaric, xenophobic Nazi Germany.

manizado la muy germánica *Historia de la literatura alemana* de A.F.C. Vilmar . . . Hasta su índice alfabético es alarmante. Ese catálogo perverso incluye unos setecientos autores, pero increíblemente silencia el nombre de Heine . . . (¡Incalculable antisemitismo el de Rohr! Le prohibe recordar el nombre de Heine en una historia de la literatura alemana, pero le permite aclamar a [the anti-Semitic writer] Rosenberg.) ("Letras alemanas: una exposición afligente," pp. 66–67).

Though Borges was incensed by the mutilation of German culture through the omission of the many Jewish writers he knew and esteemed (a long list appears in the article), it is the elimination of Heine that bothers him most. That is so because of Heine's stature in German literature, and also because the author of the *Lyrisches Intermezzo*—whose nightingales and ironies introduced him to German—is in Borges's view the prototypic German-Jewish writer, the embodiment of all the David Jerusalems condemned as he was to the "painful / Destiny of being a man and a Jew" (*OC*, 914).[16]

Borges's posture vis-à-vis the mind of Israel, is conveyed in a third story from the period, "La muerte y la brújula" (*OC*, 499–507). The fiction, which appeared in 1942, does not deal directly with the Teutonic onslaught on the Jewish representatives of Occidental culture and, unlike "Deutsches Requiem" and "El milagro secreto," does not revolve around a contest between a Nazi and a Jew. The form this narration takes is that of a detective story, specifically, a parodic reworking of the classic detective story, with Borges reversing some of its conventions.[17] One of the essential ways in which

---

[16] See Borges's comments on Heine in his prologue to *Exposición de obras de autores judíos de habla alemana* (Buenos Aires: Museo Judío de Buenos Aires, 1973), p. 10. Heine is also alluded to in "Torres Villaroel," *Inquisiciones*, p. 13; "Libros y autores extranjeros," *El Hogar*, 5 Aug. 1938, p. 24; and "Al idioma alemán," *OC*, 1116.

[17] See on Borges's opening up and parodying the detective story in "La muerte y la brújula" María Luisa Bastos, "Literalidad y transposición: 'Las repercusiones incalculables de lo verbal,' " *Revista iberoamericana*, 43, No. 100–101 (1977), 535–547. Enrique Anderson Imbert's essay, "Chesterton en

"La muerte y la brújula" must be read, then, is as an opening up by Borges of a consecrated literary mode. But such a reading does not exhaust the fiction's possibilities. Because the tale is—in Borges's own description—"a Jewish one,"[18] with a plot constructed out of the stuff of Jewish mysticism and philosophy, with comments deriding the kind of anti-Semitism rampant at the time,[19] and with Jews and Hebraists exercising their intelligence, it can likewise be read as yet another salute by the author to Hitler's hated Jew-as-Mind. "La muerte y la brújula" is, in fact, a version and perversion of certain schemes produced by that mind as part of the impossible, but inevitable human struggle to comprehend the universe. In the fiction, Borges pays tribute to—even as he exposes the limitations of—Baruch Spinoza's rational-geometric elucidation of God, humanity and cosmos. Through an homage which is at the same time a challenge, he shows his debt to this incarnation of the intellectual Jew archetype, a thinker who, he says, has greatly influenced his work.[20]

The Spinoza (or Spinozist) in "La muerte y la brújula" is Erik Lönnrot. He is the detective attempting to solve the series of three murders occurring in a nightmare version of Buenos Aires which forms the core of the story's plot. Lönnrot is what the Nazis would have called a *weisser Jude*: an intellectual; a man unafraid become a Hebraist in order to carry out his investigation (*OC*, 500); someone who shows respect for

Borges" in *El realismo mágico y otros ensayos* (Caracas: Monte Avila, 1976), pp. 53–101 is also useful for relating "La muerte y la brújula" to the detective-story tradition. Borges discusses his interest in the genre in Vázquez, pp. 117–23; and his lecture, "El cuento policial" in *Borges, oral* (Buenos Aires: Emecé-Belgrano, 1979), pp. 63–80.

   [18] "Commentaries: 'Death and the Compass,' " *The Aleph and Other Stories*, p. 269.

   [19] Bastos points out the importance of the background against which the story was written in her study, pp. 542–43.

   [20] See Borges's comments to Oded Sverlik, "Borges habla de Israel y los judíos," p. 3. Borges also discusses the importance of Spinoza in "Jorge Luis Borges: desayuno *more geometrico* (entrevista de Enrique Krauze)" in *Vuelta* (México), 3, No. 29 (April 1979), 28–31.

Jewish belief and appreciation for rabbinic and kabbalistic writings. (This, in contrast to his colleague, the probably not-insignificantly Germanic Inspector Franz Treviranus, who is repulsed by intellectualism and Judaic literature.) Lönnrot's connection to the philosopher for whom, as Borges notes, the universe was logical and hence capable of rational explanation is insinuated in "La muerte y la brújula" through a number of hints ("Baruch Spinoza," *Conferencias*, p. 107). The most obvious of these, appearing towards the middle of the story, is a letter signed "Baruj Spinoza" [sic] which is received by Treviranus, but is clearly intended for Lönnrot, who alone seems to understand it. This obvious clue serves to supplement and confirm others, which begin to appear in the narration right from the outset.

In the first paragraph the reader is told that Lönnrot prides himself on being a "pure reasoner" (*OC*, 499). This means that he tries to puzzle out the solutions to mysteries such as the one before him through abstract reasoning, ignoring "mere circumstances"—empirical evidence which is not logically deduced—and instead seeking a rational explanation for, or an organized pattern in the events (*OC*, 504).[21] Lönnrot makes this approach of a pure logician—Spinoza's approach—clear in an exchange with Treviranus after the first killing in the series, that of the rabbi and Talmudist, Marcelo Yarmolinsky. When the inspector, the antagonist of Judaic mental constructs, suggests that the homicide may have been quite simply an error, with Yarmolinsky the unwitting victim of a jewel thief who entered his hotel suite by mistake, Lönnrot retorts that his hypothesis is too fraught with chance. The death of a rabbi requires a purely rabbinic—logical, Talmudic

---

[21] In making Lönnrot use the approach of a pure logician, Borges is also following the detective-story tradition initiated by Poe, whose Auguste Dupin (mentioned by Borges in "La muerte y la brújula") solved mysteries through an "intellectual process" ("El cuento policial," p. 72). There is likewise the influence of Chesterton and his detective, Father Brown. See "Entretiens avec James E. Irby," p. 396. These sources complement the Spinozism of the story.

—explanation, not the imaginary misadventures of some imaginary robber (*OC*, 500).

Lönnrot's argument is Spinozist in its insistence that knowledge—finding out who the murderer is—can be derived from a coherent structure of premises and conclusions based on reason, and not on un-reason: improvisation, chance, circumstantial evidence and, above all, the imagination. As G. H. R. Parkinson writes in his *Spinoza's Theory of Knowledge*:

> [The philosopher believed that the] . . . search for truth was to be put upon a new and sound basis; men were no longer to go about their researches in a more or less haphazard manner, but were to do so methodically, in accordance with some plan.[22]

This plan or method, Parkinson goes on, was rooted in "the assumption that knowledge constitutes a deductive system" (p. 13). The information and ideas on which such a system was to be built could be provided only by "pure reason" (p. 15), since Spinoza considered "the imagination [the name he gave to cognition not rationally deduced] to be defective as a means of knowledge" (p. 156).

The Spinozism of Lönnrot's search for truth becomes even clearer when Borges intimates that not only its method (reason), but also its goal corresponds to the philosopher's: to reach God, who in the story as in Spinoza's system represents complete understanding of the universe under the aspect of eternity. Borges suggests this correspondence by establishing a link between the name of the assassin Lönnrot is pursuing and the ineffable Name of God (*OC*, 501; 504). At the site of each of the three homicides the pure logician is investigating, a clue is left which seems to relate the killing to a search by a Jewish sect for God's secret Name. Lönnrot, convinced that by following this lead he would discover the identity (name) of the criminal, himself becomes one of the "seekers of the Name," in effect, a seeker of God (*OC*, 501).[23] That his pursuit

---

22 G. H. R. Parkinson, *Spinoza's Theory of Knowledge* (London: Oxford University Press, 1954), p. 8.
23 A penetrating discussion of "La muerte y la brújula" as a fable of a man trying to reach God and understand the cosmos is found in D. P.

is synonymous with a pursuit of complete understanding of the universe under the aspect of eternity is made evident when Borges explains that the hidden Name Lönnrot is after contains God's ninth attribute, eternity, that is, immediate knowledge of all past, present and future things (*OC*, 501). It is also made evident by the fact that when Lönnrot finally finds his "God," under the guise of the gangster Red Scharlach (who is of Jewish background, like the Judeo-Christian Lord, and inhabits the Southside, the blurry frontier of the city which in Borges's works connotes the frontier of the soul[24]), he learns that this deity is in fact characterized by eternity and omniscience: he has emotions as wide as the endless, eternal cosmos, and knows unpublicized, hidden details about the murders and the investigation that only an all-seeing being could know (Gallagher, p. 102).

Additional indications of the fact that Lönnrot is indeed following Spinoza's tracks, that in the story's metaphysical stratum he is reproducing the Dutch-Jewish logician's project, are found in the letter signed "Baruj Spinoza" which is sent to Inspector Treviranus:

> Este recibió, la noche del primero de marzo, un imponente sobre sellado. Lo abrió: el sobre contenía una carta firmada *Baruj Spinoza* y un minucioso plano de la ciudad, arancado notoriamente de un Baedeker. La carta profetizaba que el tres de marzo no habría un cuarto crimen [the three crimes under investigation had been committed, respectively, on the third of December, January and February], pues la pinturería del Oeste, la taberna de la Rue de Toulon y el Hôtel du Nord [the sites of the murders] eran 'los vértices perfectos de un triángulo equilátero y místico'; el plano demostraba en tinta roja la regularidad de ese triángulo. Treviranus leyó con

---

Gallagher, "Jorge Luis Borges" in *Modern Latin American Literature* (New York and London: Oxford University Press, 1973), pp. 102–05. Gallagher does not discuss the Spinozist aspect of the story, but some of his insights were useful to me in developing my own analysis.

[24] Consult Barrenechea, *Labyrinth Maker*, p. 28. In constructing Scharlach as a Jewish gangster, Borges seems to have been inspired not only by theological considerations, but also—on the level of the detective story which "La muerte y la brújula" is—by the figure of Monk Eastman, the Jewish gangster he wrote about in *Historia universal de la infamia* ("El proveedor de iniquidades Monk Eastman," *OC*, 311–15).

resignación ese argumento *more geometrico* y mandó la carta y el plano a casa de Lönnrot—indiscutible merecedor de tales locuras. Erik Lönnrot las estudió. Los tres lugares, en efecto, eran equidistantes. Simetría en el tiempo (3 de diciembre, 3 de enero, 3 de febrero); simetría en el espacio, también . . . Sintió, de pronto, que estaba por descifrar el misterio. (*OC*, 503)

The letter meant for Lönnrot suggests that the key to deciphering the mystery (finding the murderer; reaching God; understanding the universe) lay in following a geometrized, mystic map; that is, a map which "demonstrated"—the word is important here—the shape of God or the cosmos.[25] The Spinozism of this is so unmistakable that Borges appended the philosopher's name to the letter. For the distinguishing features of the Amsterdam thinker's system were precisely its "geometric form" and its "unfolding of a picture of the world in the form of demonstrations and propositions."[26] That is why, in other texts, Borges refers to Spinoza as the "geometer of the divine," or as the rationalist whose major work, the *Ethics*, is peppered with axioms, postulates and definitions.[27]

Another aspect of Spinoza's geometry of the divine revealed in the letter is the idea that God, who has an infinite number of attributes, is knowable to people only through two of them: thought and extension, or time and space ("Baruch Spinoza," *Conferencias*, p. 109). After studying Baruj Spinoza's message, Lönnrot notices that the map it delineates, the map leading to the Omniscient (Scharlach, who is the true author of

---

[25] Borges indicates that the map sketched out in the letter has cosmic proportions when he says that one point could stand for Iceland; another for Mexico; a third for Hindustan (*OC*, 483). The fact that the true shape of the cosmic map Lönnrot has to follow is rhomboid, and not triangular—as the letter implies—does not invalidate the geometric *modus operandi* or the goal—God. The "equilateral and mystical triangle" is derived from Spinoza's *Ethics*, I, 17: "From the infinite nature of God . . . all things . . . flow . . . in the same way as it follows from the nature of a triangle from eternity to eternity, that its three angles are equal to two right angles" (Quoted in Will Durant, *The Story of Philosophy* [New York: Washington Square Press, 1961], p. 173).

[26] Richard H. Popkin, "Spinoza, Baruch," *Encyc. Judaica*, XV, 279.

[27] "Libros y autores extranjeros," *El Hogar*, 20 Aug. 1937, p. 76.; "Baruch Spinoza," *Conferencias*, p. 106. See, also, the poem "Baruch Spinoza," *OC*, 930.

the letter), has symmetry in time and symmetry in space (*OC*, 503). God reveals Himself spacially (at the site of each crime) and temporally (at the time of each crime), plotting out a chart of His universe which, in Spinoza's (Lönnrot's) view, unravels the mystery, makes the world intelligible to those who would study it by the light of reason.

When he lectured on the Dutch-Sephardi philosopher, Borges noted that despite Spinoza's frugal, almost indigent life, a life empty of woman's love and marred by ostracism and ill health, the philosopher was a happy man because there is no greater joy than the exercise of one's intelligence ("Baruch Spinoza," *Conferencias*, p. 106). Borges expresses his admiration for this intelligence by turning the Spinozist system into a philosophical underpinning of "La muerte y la brújula" and by making Lönnrot into a Spinoza-figure. What Borges esteems most in the rationalist from Amsterdam is the fact that he applied his vast intellectual powers to the task of answering humankind's Ultimate Questions, for in Borges's view "there is something splendid in the spectacle of men striding out to explain the universe" (Gallagher, p. 113). But the writer's tribute to the logician's mind and mission in no way constitutes an endorsement of his world-view or of his solution to the enigmas of existence. On the contrary, Borges opens the lecture in which he celebrates the Sephardi-Dutch thinker's genius by expressing doubt about the validity of Spinoza's system ("Baruch Spinoza," *Conferencias*, p. 103). In "La muerte y la brújula" he gives narrative substance to this disclaimer, questioning the very scheme he had found so magnificent as a construct of the human intellect in search of Meaning.

Borges's Spinoza, Erik Lönnrot, does not find Meaning; neither does he achieve blessedness, the contented life the philosopher believed would flow from a rational understanding of Nature. Instead of guiding him to knowledge and happiness, pure logic confronts him with error and death: his reasoned deductions do not provide the solution to the mystery since they are to a large extent wrong; and the geometry of the divine he has followed does not map out a path to a rational god who endows man with infinite wisdom, but rather to an irrational deity who weaves a labyrinth, a death

137

trap, for those mortals presumptuous enough to believe that their intellect can pierce the great *ignoramus*.[28]

But even if Spinoza's scheme, Lönnrot's scheme, fails as an absolute explanation of the Absolute, it succeeds as a provisional explanation, the only type available to humankind. That is why in "La muerte y la brújula" Borges *does* give his Spinozist detective credit for his keenness of mind and for his partial, approximate penetration of the enigma (*OC*, 499). That is why, too, he repeatedly invokes Spinoza's masterful name, lauding this incarnation of the Jew-as-Intellect, who despite his very human nothingness took on the Infinite, producing a brilliant geometry which may not explain God or Nature, but which may help people bear its impenetrability (*OC*, 200). That is why, in the final analysis, he admires all the personifications of the Jew-as-Mind mentioned here. For each, descended from those who created one of the essential human schemes sustaining Western woman in her confrontation with God's secret dictionary (*OC*, 708), himself created some admirable scheme—a literature crafted out of dreams, a poetry of images and melodies—which imposes temporary order and gives comfort in the face of the chaotic and the unintelligible.

C. The Jewish Gaucho

Just as the gaucho is Argentina's "vast generic figure" and his exploits are the backbone of the nation's most potent national myth, so the *gaucho judío* is Jewish Argentina's larger-than-life archetype, and his deeds are the core of an ethnic saga Argentine Jews consider uniquely their own.

In both cases, a book has served to embody and promote the paradigmatic figure and his story: José Hernández's poem *El gaucho Martín Fierro* (1872) for the Argentine people as a

---

[28] The theme of a Spinoza-figure who believes in a rational world only to be ultimately confronted and defeated by an irrational Power is taken up again in one of Borges's more recent stories, "Tigres azules," *Rosa y azul* (Madrid: Sedmay, 1977), n.pag.

whole; Alberto Gerchunoff's collection of stories *Los gauchos judíos* (1910), for Argentines of Jewish extraction.[1]

Borges, ever devoted to working with those symbols that awaken the collective memory, has manipulated the gaucho archetype extensively, glossing the saga of the pampa horseman and its consecrated, Hernandian version in stories, poems, essays and introductory studies.[2] Many of these texts contain a celebration of the pampa horseman, his nomadic, primitive life riding and driving cattle on the open spaces; his free spirit, inimicable to the yoke of the law and devoted to the cult of courage; his skill with the knife, an expression of that cult; his loyalty to those he admired; and his poetry, sung to the rhythm of guitar strings. When Borges writes in this vein (as in the poem "Los gauchos," *OC*, 1001), he comes closest to reaffirming the gaucho as national mythos. He seems to participate in the hero-worship of the plains rider propounded by writers like Lugones or Güiraldes for whom the gaucho qualities and activities mentioned above constituted the quintessence of *argentinidad*. Yet this is only a partial and thus erroneous picture. What would appear to be Borges's gauchophilia is tempered in other texts, when he writes, for example, that gauchesque literature—an invention of *urban* writers—has exaggerated the importance of the gaucho.[3]

---

[1] Gerchunoff's stories, which first appeared separately in *La Nación*, were published under the title *Los gauchos judíos* in 1910. The first edition of the book (La Plata: Joaquín Sesé) was prologued by the well-known nativist writer Martiniano Leguizamón. I have used the edition published in Buenos Aires by EUDEBA, 1964.

[2] Some of these glosses are: stories—"El fin" and "Biografía de Tadeo Isidoro Cruz (1829–74)," *OC*, 519–21 and 561–63; poems—"Los gauchos" and "El gaucho," *OC*, 1001 and 1111; essays—"La poesía gauchesca," *OC*, 179–197; introductory studies—Borges prologued three editions of *Martín Fierro* (Buenos Aires: Sur, 1962; Buenos Aires: Centurión, 1962; and Buenos Aires: Santiago Rueda, 1968). He also wrote forewords to Hilario Ascasubi's *Paulino Lucero, Aniceto el Gallo* and *Santos Vega* (Buenos Aires: EUDEBA, 1960), and to Estanislao del Campo's *Fausto* (Buenos Aires: Nova, 1946; Buenos Aires: Edicom, 1969). (All these studies are reprinted in *Prólogos*, pp. 89–99; 17–21; 28–31.) Another introductory study is the prologue to *Poesía gauchesca*, an anthology edited by Borges with Adolfo Bioy Casares (México: Fondo de Cultura Económica, 1955).

[3] Introduction to Sarmiento's *Facundo* (Buenos Aires: Ateneo, 1974), rpt. in *Prólogos*, p. 136.

This same interplay of homage moderated by challenge characterizes Borges's attitude to *Martín Fierro*. For instance, in "Biografía de Tadeo Isidoro Cruz (1829–1874)," which is a celebrative expansion of an episode from Hernández's poem, Borges lauds the work in the highest terms as a distinguished work, which lends itself to infinite recreation (*OC*, 561). Such acclaim quickly turns into censure, however, when the gauchesque masterpiece is made out to be a holy writ or a sacred history.[4]

All in all, Borges's attitude to the gaucho and his myth can perhaps be described as qualified acceptance: an awareness that the pampa horseman represents an intrinsic part of the Argentine ethnos and that Hernández's poem, capturing this, became Argentina's most enduring work (*OC*, 267); yet, at the same time, a refusal to canonize the gaucho or *Martín Fierro*, turning them into the be-all and end-all of Argentineity.

But if Borges's attitude towards the gaucho archetype and Hernández's text is qualified acceptance, realization held in check by transgression, his posture vis-à-vis the generic figure of the *gaucho judío* and Gerchunoff's book (which he knew well) is unadulterated transgression. While others can speak of the new, manly figure of the Jewish gaucho,[5] Borges categorically denies that such a personage even existed (*OC*, 1029). And while others can praise the story collection by Gerchunoff as the master text of Judeo-Argentine literature,[6] Borges's comments on the work generally point out that its very title is a misnomer as the Jewish immigrants Gerchunoff was writing about were farmers, not cowboys (Sorrentino, p. 36)

This transgressive position is made clear in the two stories where Borges handles the Jewish gaucho topos: "El indigno" (*OC*, 1029–33), and "Las formas de la gloria."[7] Though these selections and the emblematic character they

---

[4] Prologue to *Martín Fierro* in *Prólogos*, p. 96.

[5] Martiniano Leguizamón, prologue to the first edition of *Los gauchos judíos*, p. xi.

[6] Lázaro Schallman, *Los pioneros de la colonización judía en la Argentina* (Buenos Aires: Ejecutivo Sudamericano del Congreso Judío Mundial, 1969), p. 48.

[7] Jorge Luis Borges and Adolfo Bioy Casares, *Nuevos cuentos de Bustos Domecq*, p. 117–28.

deal with are, so to speak, a drop in the Judeo-Borgesian bucket, much more full of Bible, Kabbalah and intellectual Jews, they still merit attention. They represent Borges's response to the ethnic myth of Argentine Jewry, and it is worth considering why the author, who has reacted favorably to other Jewish paradigmatic types and tales, is so vehement in his rejection of this figure and fable, products of his own national environment. Also, in dealing with the *gaucho judío*, a would-be blend of two prototypes important in Borges, these stories illuminate the author's thoughts on each of them, and why, in view of these thoughts, gaucho and Jew cannot blend. Finally, taken in conjunction with the other Judaic strands in the fabric of his *oeuvre*, the Jewish gaucho according to Borges helps round out and clarify the total Jew according to Borges.

The term *gaucho judío* made its appearance in the story "El poeta," one of the twenty-five narrations which constitute Gerchunoff's 1910 volume. It is used to describe Favel Duglach, a resident of Rajil, a Jewish colony founded at the turn of the century in Argentina's Entre Ríos province. Duglach is a farmer, part of a group of poor, persecuted Russian Jews (Gerchunoff among them) who had come to Argentina thanks to the efforts of the Judeo-Belgian philanthropist, Baron Maurice de Hirsch. In the agricultural colonies established under his auspices, Jews like Duglach, all merchants and craftsman in Europe, were transformed into tillers of the soil, having to adapt to a rural way of life far removed from the one they knew in the Old World.[8] The result of their adaptation to the pampa was what Gerchunoff called the *gaucho judío*, a new ethnic type best exemplified by Duglach. In "El poeta," Gerchunoff describes the colonist this way:

> En su espíritu se habían fundido las tradiciones hebreas y gauchas. Aquel judío, flaco y amarillo como una llama, sentía la poesía criolla del valor en la misma forma que se exaltaba al relatar, ante el auditorio acostumbrado, algún episodio de la Biblia . . . Era una

---

[8] On the Baron de Hirsch settlements in Argentina see, Haim Avni's study (in Hebrew) *Argentine, the Promised Land* (Jerusalem: The Magnes Press, 1973); Spanish ed., *Argentina y la historia de la inmigracion judía (1810–1950)* (Buenos Aires: Universitaria Magnes, 1983).

figura original. Su garfiuda nariz se extendía por todo el rostro. Larga melena y largas barbas le daban prestancia fantástica; las bombachas y el requintado chambergo exageraban aún más su absurda silueta. Rabí Favel solía decir:

—Soy un gaucho judío . . . (p. 82)

Gerchunoff's description makes it clear that Duglach, the Jewish "gaucho," is really an acculturated foreigner whose settlement on the pampa had made him adopt certain of the native ways, and develop an appreciation for many of the local traditions. Gerchunoff's entire volume is, in fact, a chronicle of this process of acculturation, which he himself underwent. But did such assimilation into the new environment make Duglach and his fellow colonists gauchos?

In Gerchunoff's delineation of the thin, yellow Jew he writes that Duglach had a deep feeling for the native poetry of valor, that poetry which—as he adds later in the passage—extolled the nomadic life and heroism of the gaucho (p. 82). Such exaltation of the pampa heritage lies at the heart of the immigrant's gaucho identity and is underlined more than his adoption of any other of the indigenous ways (clothing, for instance). The curious thing is, however, that the heritage the immigrant glorifies in order to show his gaucho credentials belongs to a period previous to his arrival on the pampa. The heroic age of the pampa horseman, the one that gave Argentina its essential figure and fable, was over when foreigners like Duglach settled the prairies. The greenhorns of Rajil, sublimate though they might the gaucho ethos that was, actually represented not its continuation but its antithesis: their sedentary, orderly existence on bordered farms went against the very grain of what had been the gaucho's distinctive way of life. The truth was that Duglach and other immigrants had come to the plains to seal the prairie rider's death decree, rather than to perpetuate his ways because he had become dispensable in an Argentina whose shift from a pastoral to an agricultural economy called for law-abiding farmers instead of unrestrained cowboys.[9]

---

[9] Consult on this, Ricardo Rodríguez Molas, *Historia social del gaucho* (Buenos Aires: Ediciones Marú, 1968), p. 491 ff.

The term *gaucho judío* is, therefore, a misnomer, a bending of historical reality and a transgression of the pampa horseman archetype. Borges's objections to the Jewish gaucho are based in part on this misappropriation of gaucho figure, a point which both "Las formas de la gloria" and "El indigno" make clear. In the first story, a Borges-Bioy Casares collaboration written in the characteristic H. Bustos Domecq tongue-in-cheek style, a graduate student tells of his interview with author Clodomiro Ruiz, whose works are the subject of his doctoral dissertation. Ruiz is from Entre Ríos, the site of the Jewish colonies. He owes much of his literary reputation to a volume called *Querencias judías* (roughly, *Jewish Native Haunts*), famous for being a paean to the Russo-Jewish immigrants to the pampa. (The parallels with Gerchunoff's background and the work for which he gained renown are obvious.) But, as Ruiz reveals to the astonished doctoral candidate, the fame of *Querencias judías* is the result of a printing error. The original title, *Querencias juídas* (*Vanished Native Haunts*), was jumbled up by the printer, and, consequently, Ruiz, who in fact cannot stand the sight of Jews and, as the title of the book indicates, wanted to lament the disappearance of the gaucho and his pampa, became the "bard" of the settlements (p. 125). The student, unable to believe his own ears, has this exchange with the author after the dramatic revelation:

—Pero ¿cómo? ¿El señor no es un gaucho judío?
—Es como hablar con la pared. ¿No acabo de aclararle el asunto? Le digo más: yo concebí mi libro como un mazazo contra esos chacareros y mercachifles que arriaron con el gaucho de ley, sin consentirle ni un resuello. (p. 126)

The dialogue, set within a story which suggests that Gerchunoff's *gauchos judíos* are pure humbug, just like Ruiz's *Querencias judías*, indicates why Borges feels this way: the immigrants in the colonies were farmers who sold their produce and lacked the gaucho's distinguishing characteristic: a primitive type of cattle ranching (*OC*, 132). And their arrival on the pampa didn't help the true gaucho; it did him in.

The same objection to the *gaucho judío* is voiced by Borges in "El indigno." Here his mouthpiece is the protagonist, Santiago Fischbein, a Russo-Jewish immigrant to the pampa who moved to Buenos Aires in his youth and now owns a bookstore in the city. Towards the beginning of the tale, in which he recounts an episode from his adolescence, Fischbein says the following:

> No sé si ya lo he dicho alguna otra vez que soy entrerriano. No diré que éramos gauchos judíos; gauchos judíos no hubo nunca. Éramos comerciantes y chacareros. (*OC*, 1029)

As the story develops, this major argument for the nonexistence of Jewish cowboys is reinforced and fleshed out by related ones. Borges suggests that Jews like Fischbein not only lacked the plains horseman's typical pastoral way of life, but also other of his distinctive traits: the cult of manly courage, and loyalty to one's fellows—often outcasts or rebels—instead of to the law. In "El indigno," Fischbein, the supposed gaucho, is a coward and an informer, betraying the good-hearted hoodlum who trusted and befriended him to the police. He thus violates two cardinal principles of the gaucho's code of honor. To emphasize this, and bolster his contention that Fischbein is not a gaucho, Borges makes his opposite, the man he delivers up to the hated authorities, a representative of the gaucho mythos. This man is the *compadrito* Francisco Ferrari, who though no more a nomadic plains rider than the Jewish immigrant, can still "feel and be felt a gaucho" because he and his men have some of the essential gaucho qualities: an animal-related profession—butcher or wagoner;[10] a strong sense of friendship; and bravery coupled with antagonism to the law (*OC*, 1031). The contrast between Fischbein and Ferrari is telling. Though both are young men when they meet in the Buenos Aires slum where they play out their story, and both are in some way connected to the gaucho, one is the antithesis of the legendary horseman, the other his urban counterpart.[11]

---

[10] In the introduction to *Poesía gauchesca* Borges writes that the urban day laborer—the water carrier, wagon driver or slaughterer—was essentially no different from the gaucho (p. vii).

[11] While "El indigno" presents the thesis and antithesis of the gaucho myth, in the typical, multilayered Borges fashion it can also be read as a replay

The question that now comes to mind is, didn't Gerchunoff, a man who had lived in the Baron de Hirsch pampa colonies, know that Jews like Duglach or Fischbein were (as Borges argues) the very opposites of the gaucho? The evidence of his book shows that he did. The most obvious indication is his description of Don Remigio Calamaco, an old—true—cowboy who befriended and helped the Jewish settlers. Calamaco is always seen on horseback; he assists the colonists only in tasks involving livestock, not in any agricultural work; he is a veteran of civil wars and knife duels; and he obeys the law of macho courage over the law of the land, ending his days in jail after stabbing his own son for being a *maula*, a coward. In addition, he feels hemmed-in in the colony, and looks upon the colonists plowing their land and counting their chickens with "hidden melancholy" (p. 44).

Given this clear understanding of the dissonance between the gaucho and the so-called *gaucho judío*, why did Gerchunoff choose to misappropriate the plain rider's figure for his fellow Judeo-Russian immigrants? The answer to this question is important in a discussion of Borges's negative reaction to the Jewish "gaucho," because the motive that led Gerchunoff to transform Jewish greenhorns into Argentine cowboys is apparently another of Borges's motives for rejecting this transformation.

Gerchunoff's work appeared in 1910, the year which marked the centennial of Argentina's independence. It was a time for affirming all that would extol, sublimate and glorify Argentineity. [12] And who was more representative of that Argentineity than the gaucho? He thus became the ideal national symbol around which all Argentines could rally. Those who came of Hispano-Creole background, descendents of the original Spanish settlers, were particularly interested in extolling

---

of an even older myth: the Jesus/Judas story (which is itself a replay of the Cain and Abel myth). Fischbein is the betrayer of Ferrari, who was to him a god (*OC*, 1031). This interpretation is given by McMurray, pp. 110–11.

[12] On the centennial and the reaffirmation of Argentineity see David Viñas, *Literatura argentina y realidad política: apogeo de la oligarquía*, pp. 165–166, 178–79.

him because he belonged to what they considered the "authentic" Argentina, the pastoral-patriarchal pampa society which they controlled and which was quickly vanishing under the pressure of new European immigration and urbanization. It was indeed thanks to the efforts of the Creole establishment and its supporters that "gaucho" came to equal "Argentina," and *Martín Fierro* became the national epic.

But Argentines of greenhorn stock were no less interested in singing the gaucho's praises. These newcomers, anxious to be considered full-fledged citizens, and aware that the pampa horseman had become the symbol of the nation, also celebrated him. By identifying with the maximum emblem of nationhood they thought, they would be made an integral part of the Argentine people. [13]

Gerchunoff's *Los gauchos judíos* is one example of this line of thinking. His motive was clearly captured by Bernardo Verbitsky, another Judeo-Argentine writer, when he noted that Argentina's Jews received their citizenship papers with this book. [14] To this day, the *gaucho judío* is cited as proof of the Jews' total adaptation to Argentina. In imitations, reelaborations and movie versions the story of the Jewish "cowboys" is honored as the epic of the new life, of the possession of the new homeland. [15] Even those who would attempt to desacralize the myth, arguing that the history of Argentine Jewry subsequent to 1910 betrayed the promise of their total adaptation into Argentina's society, would agree that Gerchunoff captured the essence of Argentine Jewry's collective experience and dilemma: that of *gringos* striving to be *gauchos*, of a

---

[13] On the significance of the gaucho for immigrants and Hispano-Creoles consult Gladys S. Onega, *La inmigración en la literatura argentina, 1880–1910*, p. 36 ff.

[14] "Premio Alberto Gerchunoff," *Comentario*, 12, No. 44 (1965), 86. I discuss the background and significance of Gerchunoff's book further in my article, "Alberto Gerchunoff: ¿gaucho judío o antigaucho europeizante?"

[15] See, for example, Bernardo León Pecheny, *Tierra gaucha* (Buenos Aires: Acervo Cultural, 1975); and Susana Goldemberg, *Cuentos de la bobe* (Santa Fe: Liberia Colmegua, 1976). In 1975, a movie version of Gerchunoff's book premiered in Buenos Aires.

religio-cultural minority of foreign origin seeking to come to terms with its Argentine environment. [16]

The *gaucho judío* is, then, the Jew naturalized and provincialized, linked to a patriotic myth in an attempt to show complete accommodation to one patrimony and one place. But this image of the Jew is the exact opposite of Borges's vision of him, and herein appears to lie another of his objections to Gerchunoff's figure and fable. As mentioned earlier, Borges rejects the chauvinistic myth with which the Jewish gaucho is associated. And this antinationalistic attitude vis-à-vis the plains rider can only be heightened when it comes to his Jewish "version." For if the gaucho cannot be a patriotic emblem, the Jew-disguised-as-gaucho can be even less since to Borges, the Jew is the cosmopolitan antithesis of all nationalism. To drive this point home, Borges says the following of Santiago Fischbein, his would-be Jewish gaucho:

Firme y tranquilo, solía condenar el sionismo, que haría del judío un hombre común, atado, como todos los otros, a una sola tradición y un solo sitio, sin las complejidades y discordias que ahora lo enriquecen. (*OC*, 1029)

Gerchunoff, through his linking of the Jew to a nationalistic archetype had wanted to show that he *could* be tied down territorially and culturally. As a way of emphasizing this, his book compares Argentina to Zion, the Promised Land on which the Jew would shed his rootlessness and become an "ordinary" man, uninational, and hence unicultural (pp. 21, 30). But Borges dislikes that image of the Jew, and he makes his feelings clear in the words from "El indigno," which also outlines the counterimage, the Jew the way Borges likes him. In the course of the story of Santiago Fischbein this contrast between the (negative) Gerchunoffian image and the (posi-

---

[16] Consult on this, Saúl Sosnowski, "Contemporary Jewish-Argentine Writers: Tradition and Politics," *Latin American Literary Review*, 6, No. 12 (1978) pp. 1–14; rptd. Robert and Roberta Kalechofsky, ed. *Echad: An Anthology of Latin American Jewish Writings* (Marblehead, Mass.: Michah Publications, 1980), 16–18, 27; and Leonardo Senkman, *La identidad judía en la literatura argentina* (Buenos Aires: Editorial Pardes, 1983), pp. 17 ff.

tive) Borgesian counterimage is reiterated. When measured up against the gaucho virtues of the nationalistic myth, Fischbein is a failure; but when he becomes an internationalist, the owner of a book store (remember that for Borges the universe equals the library), and the purveyor of world literature on the Buenos Aires scene (he sells volumes on the Kabbalah and is an anthologist of Spinoza), Fischbein is a success: he enjoys his work, has a good social position, a fine family and friends. He is also, significantly, a good Argentine and a good Jew having found his place in Argentine society not by turning into a "gaucho," but by exemplifying and fostering cultural complexity, which for Borges is the hallmark of good Argentineity *and* good Jewishness (*OC*, 1030).

In "La Strátegie de la forme" Laurent Jenny writes that the essence of intertextuality is always "une vocation critique, ludique et exploratoire." (p. 281). These words apply perfectly to Borges's handling of *Los gauchos judíos*. Borges criticizes and mocks the book, laying bare what he considers its incongruities. This transgressive vocation is the result of an ideological gap which separates Borges from Gerchunoff. The Rajil colonist was an immigrant, a member of a homeless people eager to end its diaspora, strike territorial roots and belong to a nation. His manipulation of the gaucho mystique was a result of this condition and these needs, because when he wrote to be a gaucho meant to be of the land, to be an Argentine. Borges, on the other hand, has a very different background and hence very different beliefs. He is an Argentine-born cosmopolite and antinationalist who accepts the gaucho as a valuable and consecrated archetype, but feels no need to affect a gaucho identity to prove his patriotism; who is interested in the Jew as the paradigmatic extraterritorial culture maker, not as the hated wanderer desirous of a persecution-free land; and who is thus dissatisfied with Gerchunoff's violation of both a native symbol, the gaucho, and a universal symbol, the Jew.

Index

154

155

159

Scripta humanistica

Published Volumes

D. W. McPheeters, *Estudios humanísticos sobre la "Celestina."* $24.50.

Everett W. Hesse, *The "Comedia" and Points of View.* $24.50.

Marta Ana Diz, *Patronio y Lucanor: la lectura inteligente "en el tiempo que es turbio."* Prólogo de John Esten Keller. $26.00.

Estudios literarios en honor de Gustavo Correa. Eds. Manuel Durán, Charles Faulhaber, Richard Kinkade, T. A. Perry. $25.00.

Francisco Delicado, *Portrait of Lozana: The Exuberant Andalusian Woman.* Translation, introduction and notes by Bruno M. Damiani. $33.00.

Renaissance and Golden Age Studies in Honor of D. W. McPheeters. Ed. Bruno M. Damiani. $25.00.

James F. Jones, Jr., *The Story of a Fair Greek of Yesteryear.* A Translation from the French of Antoine-François Prévost's *L'Histoire d'une Grecque moderne.* With Introduction and Selected Bibliography. $30.00.

Colette H. Winn, *Jean de Sponde: Les sonnets de la mort ou La poétique de l'accoutumance.* Préface par Frédéric Deloffre. $22.50.

163

Paul A. Gaeng, *Collapse and Reorganization of the Latin Nominal Flection as Reflected in Epigraphic Sources.* Written with the assistance of Jeffrey T. Chamberlin. $24.00.

Salvatore Calomino, *From Verse to Prose: The Barlaam and Josaphat Legend in Fifteenth-Century Germany.* $28.00.

Jack Weiner, *"En busca de la justicia social: estudio sobre el teatro español del Siglo de oro,"* $24.50.

Edna Aizenberg, *The Aleph Weaver: Biblical, Kabbalistic and Judaic Elements in Borges.* $25.00.

Forthcoming

Carlo Di Maio, *Antifeminism in Selected Works of Enrique Jardiel Poncela.* $20.50.

Philip J. Spartano, *Giacomo Zanella: Poet, Essayist, and Critic of the "Risorgimento."* Preface by Roberto Severino. $24.00.

Juan de Mena, *Coplas de los siete pecados mortales: Second and Third Continuations.* Ed. Gladys Rivera. $25.50.

Michael G. Paulson and Tamara Alvarez-Detrell, *Cervantes, Hardy, and "La fuerza de la sangre."* $25.50.

Barbara Mujica, *Spanish Pastoral Characters.* $25.00.

Susana Hernández Araico, *La ironía en tragedias de Calderón.* $25.00.

Kent Ljungquist, *The Grand and the Fair: Poe's Landscape Aesthetics and Pictorial Techniques.* $25.00.

Vittorio Felaco, *The Poetry and Selected Prose of Camillo Sbarbaro.* Edited and Translated by Vittorio Felaco. With a Preface by Franco Fido. $25.00.